BLADE® PRESENTS

42nd Edition

Knives
2022

EDITED BY JOE KERTZMAN

Published by

Gun Digest® Books, an imprint of Caribou Media Group, LLC
Gun Digest Media
5600 W. Grande Market Drive, Suite 100
Appleton, WI 54913
gundigest.com

To order books or other products call 920.471.4522 ext. 104
or visit us online at gundigeststore.com

CAUTION: Technical data presented here, particularly technical data on handloading and on firearms adjustment and alteration, inevitably reflects individual experience with particular equipment and components under specific circumstances the reader cannot duplicate exactly. Such data presentations therefore should be used for guidance only and with caution. Caribou Media accepts no responsibility for results obtained using these data.

ISBN: 978-1-951115-42-5

Edited by Joe Kertzman and Corey Graff

Printed in the United States of America

10 9 8 7 6 5 4 3 2 1

Dedication and Acknowledgments

Like the royal armorers of yore, today's knife companies and custom makers fashioning knives for the U.S. armed forces, as well as the National Guard, Air National Guard, and allied forces, should be saluted. Edged tools and weapons makers take great pride in providing soldiers with the equipment they can use.

In modern warfare knives are more often used as tools capable of cutting cord, rope, and even wire; for busting open crates; and anything from search and rescue to evasion. They assist in building and tearing down, breaching and escaping.

Makers, designers, and developers of World War II knives included Floyd Nichols, Hoyt Buck, David Murphy, John Ek, Col. Rex Applegate, Frank Richtig, William Ewart Fairbairn, Eric Anthony Sykes, Donald W. Moore, E.W. Stone and John Nelson Cooper. Randall Knife Company, Ka-Bar, Union Cutlery Company and Case made knives for soldiers during "The Big One."

When 2019 rolled around, it marked the 75th anniversary of many significant battles that turned the tide for the Allies in World War II. That year also designated the last of the major anniversaries surviving soldiers, most of whom are well into their 90s, will see. "They obviously won't be around for the centennial celebrations in 2044," BLADE Magazine Editor Steve Shackleford pointed out in a fantastic article, "How World War II Forged the Custom Knife Industry."

Shackleford also noted, "The argument can be made that the custom knife industry traces its roots to World War II. It was during the war that such knifemakers as *BLADE* Magazine Cutlery Hall-Of-Fame® members Bo Randall, Rudy Ruana, William Scagel, M.H. Cole and Dan Dennehy made knives for the troops. Dennehy, in fact, both made knives for the troops during the war and served in it, joining the Navy in 1940 and seeing action in Saipan, the Philippines and other campaigns."

Shackleford continued, "And then there were those who used knives in the war, people such as U.S. Army Corporal Eugene 'Gene' Gutierrez of the First Special Service Force (FSSF). The FSSF carried the legendary Case V-42 dagger and was comprised of specialists in mountain climbing, skiing, demolition and airborne ops.

"Wounded eight times in combat," Shackleford explained, "Gene was with the FSSF when it scaled the 10,000-foot-high Monte la Difensa in the Italian campaign and dislodged the occupying Germans."

The climb was "pretty much straight up," Gene said of the monumental effort. It took all night under one of the heaviest artillery barrages of the war, but the Forcemen made it up the mountain and routed the enemy. Later the FSSF was inserted at Anzio, where they pushed the Germans back again.

Today's servicemen have more choices than ever in quality combat, tactical and military models made by companies such as Ontario, Ka-Bar, Spartan Blades, Emerson Knives, Strider Knives, Benchmade Knife Company, Gerber, Cold Steel, SOG Specialty Knives, Columbia River Knife & Tool, Spyderco Knife Company, Chris Reeve Knives, Fallkniven, DPX Gear, Al Mar, Case Knives, Queen Cutlery, Kershaw, United Cutlery, Zero Tolerance, Eickhorn, TOPS Knives and Fox Knives, to name a few.

The custom knifemakers fashioning knives for soldiers are too numerous to name, but rest assured, the pride in workmanship, honor, and feeling of duty those fashioning military tools and weapons experience is palpable. A conversation with any one of them reveals stories about how the knives were used, by what soldiers, of which branches of service and units, in what part of the world, and how the edges, handles and sheaths held up. Making knives for soldiers is as patriotic and humbling as manufacturing tanks or designing air and ground communications or weapons systems.

I dedicate this book to all those making knives for U.S. and allied soldiers and the military, in general, and acknowledge your dedication and patriotism. I thank you for your service in equipping our military men and women with the best tools in the world and thus helping ensure freedom and liberty for decades to come. They are certainly deserving of your talents and incredible workmanship. Thank you for fighting the good fight and for your service. □

~ Joe Kertzman

Contents

On The Cover

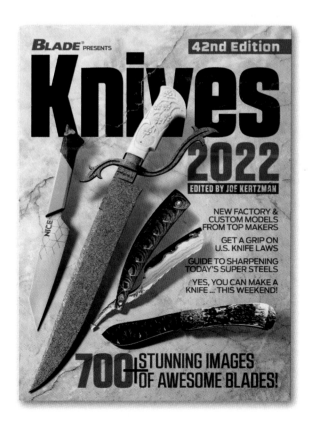

"**N**ICE" is a good word for the first of the fearsome foursome gracing the front cover of the *KNIVES 2022* book. MacKenzie Arrington, who works under the business name Nice Handmade Knives, built the "Helix Rocket Petty Knife" at the far left using vintage paper Micarta, dyed maple, and G-10 handle scales and a 15N20 high carbon steel blade. The large, sweeping S-guard bowie with the carved mammoth ivory grip in a cherry blossom motif is by none other than Paul DiStefano, who forged a wood-grain-pattern W2 damascus blade for the piece. Then there's the "Dragon" straight razor by Joe Edson, complete with a Takefu Yu-Shoku Steel blade and a Mars Valley carbon fiber handle sculpted to resemble dragon scales. At the bottom right is another absolute stunner—Bubba Crouch's Panama-style trapper dressed in a mosaic damascus blade forged by Rick Dunkerley, integral bronze beaten and cold-blued bolsters, mammoth ivory handle scales and a bronze arrowhead shield. Bill Ruple engraves even the back spring. (SharpByCoop knife photos)

Introduction

The handmade knife industry is in good shape, on solid ground and poised for a promising future. That is certainly easy for a guy who writes about the knives and makers to say—he does not have to put in the sweat equity, long hours of hard labor, investment in materials and machines, second mortgages, trips to shows, trial and error, stress and insecurity, with no set wages, benefits, health insurance or retirement plan.

No, but sometimes an outside viewpoint is needed to assure those invested that it is going to be alright. And it is.

It has not been an easy transition for seasoned bladesmiths and knifemakers to go from selling their wares at shows, taking orders, delivering knives months and sometimes years later, traveling from town to town, state to state and out of the country, to having websites, email, Facebook, Instagram and YouTube. There were no videos to show them how to make knives, their competition consisted of other makers in the next county over attending the same hammer-ins and gun or knife shows as them, and they needed to make better knives than the next guy or gal.

That last part hasn't changed—quality is still king. Everything else, it seems, has evolved. A promising young bladesmith in Yakima, Washington, can fashion a knife in her workshop, take pictures of it using her digital camera set to the "no glare" function, post the images on multiple online sites and social media pages and sell them to collectors in Ann Arbor, Michigan, or South Sudan, North Africa, and take money via PayPal, Stripe, Google Pay or Square.

So, where is the quality control? That is the million-dollar question and with no easy answers. There are some pre-knowns: in the 1950s through the '80s and even into the '90s and 2000s, countless knife deals were made on a handshake and a man's word. Most of those turned out to be honest exchanges with satisfied makers and customers. Yet, listen long enough to a couple of seasoned knifemakers talk, and you will hear about the crooks, scammers, posers and slimeballs that existed then, as now. The industry has a way of flushing them out.

What is evident to the observer is that the innovation, materials, designs and variety of handmade knives have expanded to the point of seemingly endless possibilities. New blood coming into the industry is constant, and ideas are limitless. Choices are overwhelming and navigating through them all can be challenging.

It is a vibrant, hot market. It is not easy for the buyer. There are few safeguards or guarantees, but it is a free market and a constant exchange of ideas. As soon as one innovation catches on—mosaic damascus or Timascus flipper folders—something else takes its place or at least offers a new direction—copper san mai steel or Santoku kitchen knives with Tasmanian blackwood handles.

Just when the American Bladesmith Society admits a dozen new apprentice smiths, a hammer-in takes place in Tuscaloosa, Alabama, and some kid forges a meteorite blade into a hollow-ground dagger with a mammoth tooth handle.

Therein is the saving grace—national organizations like The Knifemakers' Guild and American Bladesmith Society; renowned handmade knife shows such as the BLADE Show, ICCE, Spirit of Steel and New York Custom Knife Show; websites like BladeGallery.com or knifecenter.com; and purveyors and dealers of fine knives who have built solid reputations and can make recommendations based on experience and knowhow.

Similarly, the *KNIVES 2022* book is chockful of high-quality, innovative, finely fit and finished custom knives, with a few production pieces thrown in to satisfy all tastes and budgets. Within the Features, Trends, State of the Art and Factory Trends sections are edged tools and weapons built by the most highly regarded artisans on the planet. Fascinating articles are penned by the best knife writers working today. It is a world of knives in 300 color pages ready to be delved into and explored.

Those who appreciate knives know quality when they see it, and while there is no substitute for holding a handmade knife or a model fresh off the factory floor, the 42nd Edition of the *KNIVES* Annual book is a great way to see it all in one place, from an outsider's point of view. Herein you will discover why the handmade knife industry is in such great shape, and with no risk involved for turning the pages! □

~Joe Kertzman

2022

WOODEN SWORD AWARD

Image by Caleb Royer Photography

For the first time in decades, the Wooden Sword Award is not being given to an individual solely for the exceptional quality of their work. There is no question that the knife presented here is of exceptional quality, particularly the highly patterned meteorite blade and brilliant mammoth tooth handle, as well as the gold inlay.

The remarkable young maker behind the knife is most impressive, not only for his interest in the history of knifemaking materials but also for his enthusiastic mastery of the subject.

I will let him tell you:

"My name is Tristan Dare, and I am 17 years old. This little push dagger took roughly four weeks to make and proved itself to be a perfect challenge given the materials.

"The handle is made from stabilized mammoth tooth, dating to be roughly 20,000 years old. The blade is forged from the oldest Octahedrite meteorite ever discovered and quite possibly the oldest meteorite ever found on Earth, then topped off with a 24-karat gold inlay.

"The meteorite itself came from two planetoids that collided with each other, resulting in the iron core of one blowing up and spewing out in planet Earth's direction. For billions of years, it floated in space cooling down, in just the perfect course to find itself landing on Earth.

"It hit Earth nearly 1 million years ago B.C.E. [Before the Common Era] in the Quaternary period. Since it fell on Earth, it has survived four ice ages

until, in 1906, in the small village of Kitkiöjärvi (87 miles from the Arctic Circle), the first fragments were found. To this day, only 40 total fragments are known, some big and some small.

"The pattern displayed is 100 percent natural, and in fact 100 percent mathematical. Due to cooling over billions of years in space, the crystalline structure has relaxed from millions of sides to only eight sides, thus leaving us a definitive pattern between the nickel and the iron.

"Meteorite is quite often referred to as a 'magical' steel, not only because it is from space, but also because when it is heated, the pattern disappears. Forever. This is because of the cooling of the steel, thus creating the pattern. So, once it is heated over 900 degrees Fahrenheit, the pattern is lost. But few have experimented to try and keep the pattern.

"And that is exactly what I did. After a little help, I was able to successfully forge the meteorite, heat-treat and temper it, and keep the pattern.

"Very few blades have achieved this outcome, and I am very proud to be the maker of this piece."

You should be proud, Tristan— both you and the knife are remarkable and thus well-deserving of the 2022 Wooden Sword Award. □

~ Joe Kertzman

Animal Rescue Knives Save Lives

A committed and compassionate group uses survival knives to protect wildlife

By Greg Bean

Rock climbers, like most outdoors people, are stewards of their surroundings, the land where they tread. Just as every hunter, nature photographer or fisherman I have known is or was an environmentalist, so are climbers. I have come to appreciate that they are also healers and they carry knives as part of their kits.

This article chronicles animal rescues where a knife was an essential tool. I am a climber, so it was natural for me to reach out to climbers for this article.

LeeLoo is a crag dog. Agile and energetic, she scrambles mountain hillsides much better than the humans she adventures with. Her owner, Kaleb Greenan, has taken her on climbs since she was a pup. Kaleb is a professional educator of humans, so he has also taught her well.

She will stay close at hand when off the leash, does not object to being on a leash and waits patiently at the bottom of the cliff while the nutty humans climb all day. She carries her own pack with her food and water. On a group climb to Pilot Mountain, one highway exit from Mt. Airy, North Carolina, the inspiration for Mayberry on The Andy Griffith Show, LeeLoo was nosing around off the side of the trail when the cord used as a leash wrapped around one of her front legs.

She lost her footing and went over the edge. It was steep, not quite vertical, so three of her paws had contact with the steeply graded ground, but just barely. Her front leg was snared in the leash, getting wrenched and promising to be a dislocation if action was not quickly taken. She was yelping and fighting against the leash, which made matters worse.

Above: The finer details of Joe DiScullo's Benchmade Griptilian folder show best while displayed as if it were in a desert, and the knife looks equally good in the natural surroundings of the Arizona wilderness.
Right: Rock climber Kaleb Greenan poses by his crag dog, LeeLoo, with Kaleb's Benchmade 530 Pardue Lightweight Axis folder in the foreground. LeeLoo is unimpressed by this but still cooperative.

One of the climbers, Garret Gosset, immediately jumped over the side of the trail, losing his footing but grabbing a tree. He tried to raise LeeLoo and take the tension off her leg. Panicked and hurting, LeeLoo bit the living heck out of him. It is laughable now, but at the time, there was a punctured human as well as the endangered dog. Garret could take care of himself, though. I watched with surging adrenaline but did not know how best to help.

Cutting the Leash

On the trail, Joe DiScullo, a climber who had kept his wits about him, said to Kaleb, "I'm cutting the leash." Joe pulled his folder from his pocket and cut the rope. LeeLoo again had four legs on the ground and was able to come back up the mountainside. She was scared and feeling pain, but it was minor compared to a dislocation or broken bone that would have otherwise been in store for her.

The knife that Joe pulled was a Benchmade Griptilian. Joe says he has carried a Griptilian for more than a decade, just not always the same one as, "Airport security is my nemesis."

He has owned the mini- and full-size versions. For the LeeLoo rescue, he had a full-size model with a drop-point blade. "I've always carried a utility folder, but after that day, this will be part of my kit forever," Joe assures.

He had watched the first rescue attempt and knew a second person jumping off the trail was not the answer. The answer was his knife, cutting through the 9-millimeter rope cleanly without having to saw at it.

"A rope under tension cuts like butter," he notes. "It defused the situation immediately."

When interviewing Joe, he had such enthusiasm for the Griptilian that I expected him to have a collection of knives. Nope.

"I'm a minimalist," he allows. "Buy once, do it right and it'll last forever. I have Japanese sharpening stones, which are not cheap, but I will never have to replace them. When camping or climbing, my one knife does everything from cutting rope to clearing brush, shaving kindling and food preparation. I never skimp on quality. I want anything I own to still be perfectly fine the day before I die."

Joe DiScullo scales a cliff at Red Rocks Canyon, in Nevada, on a climb called Yaak Crack.
Photo by Chad Jones

Climbing Passion

Joe is so passionate about climbing that he moved from North Carolina to Scottsdale, Arizona, to have access to bigger mountains. He is an investment counselor for Vanguard and his work is done by computer and telephone. His office can be anywhere, and it is not always indoors.

LeeLoo's owner, Kaleb, a climber of course, also carries a Benchmade folder, a discontinued model based on Joe's recommendation—the 530 Pardue Lightweight Axis with a spear-point blade. He has had the same knife for 10 years and has not given it up to the TSA (Transportation Security Administration), but he understands how that happens.

"When carrying a knife is like carrying your house key, you don't think about it … until the buzzer goes off [at airport security]," he relates.

As its name suggests, the Lightweight Axis weighs only a few ounces, which is important to him. "When you're already carrying 30 pounds of climbing gear," Kaleb reasons, "you don't want a knife that'll pull your shorts down."

Nick Harvey and Cheryl Raines Harvey have fine-tuned the outdoor adventure life to an artform. They are both scuba divers who take part in reef preservation and rescue work. Knives are part of all divers' kits and get a regular workout removing fishing line, netting, all manner of debris and plastics embedded and fouling the reefs.

While rescues of marine life are plentiful and heartwarming, Nick and Cheryl focus on coral reefs, which are always where you expect them to be. It is not always possible to successfully locate a sea turtle or dolphin reported to be snared in a piece of netting, but a reef stays in place.

Coral reefs are gigantic villages of single-cell animals. Per Wikipedia, "A coral reef is an underwater ecosystem characterized by reef-building corals. Reefs are formed of colonies of coral polyps held together by calcium carbonate. Most coral reefs are built from stony corals, whose polyps cluster in groups."

Shark Rescue

That may sound durable, but it is a vulnerable village. Besides improving the aesthetics of a dive site, Nick and Cheryl preserve the ecosystem that starts with these single, tiny organisms and amps up through the largest of fish that are underpinned by the reef. Yep, they are saving sharks and whales.

"True," says Nick, "they are living organisms … well, until they're stifled by rubbish! We are both certified for Dive Against Debris and try and do the monthly dives to clear rubbish from the reefs. It goes without saying that we bring up anything manageable that we come across on any dive."

Dive Against Debris is a private non-profit organization that promotes and assists reef preservation and collects data used by scientists concerned with the health of the oceans, data which may turn into policy and legislation. They clean up the reefs and turn in their results to data scientists that influence legislation and funding.

When talking to Nick for this article, I wanted to learn as much as I could about scuba knives. One of the first things he said was that most divers lean towards knives with blunt tips. Stabbing yourself equates to having a bad day diving.

Divers often strap their knives to the inside of one leg to keep blades from catching on things, which might happen if secured to the outer body.

Nick is not an advocate of the "bigger is better" approach and has seen divers with knives the size of short swords. "What do you need a knife that big for? There is nothing that needs stabbing," he reasons. "If you have angered a shark so much that it attacks you, a knife won't save you. You're dead."

Nick and Cheryl live full-time as adventurers. They sold their home and all needless possessions and bought an RV (recreational vehicle) and trailer. The trailer holds their two motorcycles, ski gear, rock climbing gear, and of course, scuba gear. They traveled coast to coast climbing, hiking, trekking and skiing, and eventually made their way to Key West, which is their home now.

Dive Master Work

Nick's work is writing. He is in the middle of a nine-book series about a dive master that gets caught up in various intrigues. Titled, "The AJ Bailey Adventure Series," it combines his passion for diving, an obsession with military history and a love of the Cayman Islands. The series will stretch from 1945 to current times and is available on Amazon, of course.

Cheryl works at marketing the books and is senior office associate at the Rainbow Reef Dive Center in Key West, which means she takes reservations, handles check-ins and facilitates diver training as a liaison for PADI (Professional Association of Diving Instructors).

And they dive regularly and work at healing the coral reefs.

Mitch Rutledge climbs, guides, kayaks and gets out regularly on one of his four motorcycles. He is also a mechanical engineer with Collins Aerospace.

Mitch's story stems from elementary school, when he was an avid fisherman, a pastime he practiced frequently with family and friends. While fishing on a pier at Ft. Desoto Park just outside of Tampa, he and his friend encountered a pelican that had fishing line wrapped around its body and could not extend one wing. The pelican could walk but not fly.

"Pelicans will try to poach fish off the pier. Taking someone's catch is easier than catching their own. They would fly down and take fish as it was being reeled up to the pier. I guess the hook would be pulled out of the fish's mouth as they flew away," Mitch explains.

Something did not work out right for this bird.

The two friends tried catching the pelican to cut it free but were outmaneuvered by the bird. "We were a little scared of it, actually; it seemed as big as we were," Mitch relates.

Above: A typical multi-purpose dive knife, the Aqua Lung Small Squeeze embodies a blunt tip and a multitude of features. Its grip is designed to be secure even when wearing gloves. Left: Types of knives used in coral reef cleanup vary from a gut-hook-style cutting tool to a blunt-tip Aqua Lung Squeeze Lock designed by Blackie Collins and a titanium-blade Seac sharp dive knife.

Fishing Line Cut

Several adult bystanders saw what they were up to and caught the bird. Once hands were laid on it, Mitch cut the fishing line, stepped back, the bird was released and off it flew.

He does not remember much about the knife, and it is long gone by now, but he remembers its main use was for cutting up squid for bait.

Dr. Thomas Koch performed a rescue of one of the least cuddly animals, a snake. He uses netting around his fruit trees to keep birds from eating the fruit. Once all the fruit is picked, he removes the netting and stores it.

One year, he took a couple days to get it all done and found that the netting that was on the ground contained a black snake. It had become so entangled, there was no way it was going to get itself out. The harder it tried for forward progress, the more it became embedded in the netting.

There was only one way to free the snake; the netting would have to be cut. Out came his folder, a Victorinox, or a Swiss Army Knife to most of us. "It took me about 20 minutes. There were so many strands of the webbing I had to cut," Thomas relates, "and with the snake writhing around, I had to make sure not to cut it."

Freed Snake Never Struck

"The amazing thing is all the while I was working to free her, she never struck at me," he says. "It's as if she knew I was trying to help." I am not sure why he thought the snake was female.

Thomas, an engineering professor, carries the same knife he takes rock climbing or hiking. The Swiss Army Knife has been up the hardest climb in Europe—the north face of the Eiger—and on both Mt. Blanc and the Matterhorn, all in Switzerland where he is from.

Almost 40 years ago, Thomas took a non-climber up a Swiss mountain so he could celebrate his 50th birthday. The name of the peak is Alt Mann, which translates to Old Man. The birthday celebrant was

Above: The sheath of the Aqua Lung Small Squeeze is easily mounted to a buoyancy control device (BCD).
Left: Traditionally worn strapped to the insides of divers' legs, large dive knives come in blunt-tip and pointed versions. Blunt blades are common to avoid accidental injury.

so pleased that he gave Thomas his knife, acquired in the Swiss Army. Just as an aside, at that time, all Swiss were part of the Swiss Army. Thomas carries the same Victorinox Swiss Army Knife today.

When interviewing Thomas, he showed me his knife collection. Prized among the knives was the folder his grandfather carried, a Victorinox of course. His grandfather, born in 1895, had served in both world wars. The Swiss enforced their neutrality with more than words and had armed forces stationed at all entry points into the country. His grandfather served at a high pass at the Swiss-Italian border.

Victorinox was established, in 1884, and it is still going strong.

So are climbing, scuba diving, kayaking, fishing, RV'ing, motorcycling and adventuring in the USA, and many knives are used to free animals encountered along the way. □

IGNORE THE HYPE:

Find a Good Knife in Today's Market

Take it from someone who makes and studies knives—you can discern quality!

By Kevin Cashen,
American Bladesmith Society master smith

For as long as human beings have engaged in trade, there has been marketing, that subtle or not so subtle art of convincing buyers that you are the best choice. With any individual connected to the internet able to spotlight their awesomeness, the task of making a truly educated consumer choice is more challenging than ever.

Let's face it. When we choose a handmade blade over a production or factory model, we buy the maker as much as the knife. So, learning to examine marketing for what it also tells us about the maker can be advantageous.

Something I have noticed about truly great knifemakers is how terrible they are at the business end of things, especially self-promoting. While such artisans cannot be bothered by the distraction of marketing, they will be almost neurotic about blade details that nobody but them will ever see, allowing the work to speak for itself.

If you find one of those makers for whom reputation has replaced the need for marketing, you will probably enjoy owning their knives more than those from "famous" artisans. Never forget the difference between celebrity and reputation. One is easily contrived, and the other is well earned.

Makers who are still building reputations will want to spotlight the quality of their knives, but always remember that doing what it was meant to do,

The author regularly watches Tim Zowada fret over tolerances less than .0001 inch in his work, but it shows.

Bill Wiggins is an avid hunter with a lifetime of using knives in the field to guide him in making good ones.

Mert Tansu has knife skills from years in a kitchen to guide his exceptional skills at making them.

Rick Marchand is one maker who fashions an honest outdoor knife, ready for hard use.

very well, is the only real testament of a quality blade. They may know how to forge, grind or heat treat, but does the maker have a good understanding of intended use? Is an artist who has never left Manhattan the right person to make you the ultimate hunter or bushcraft knife? Is the outdoor survivalist who has never set foot in a kitchen the one to make your dream Gyuto chef's knife?

More importantly, does the knifemaker understand the essentials of a superior cutting tool? After a lifetime of studying blades, inside and out, I have distilled a well-functioning knife down to what I call the edge performance triangle. The three factors of "steel selection," "geometry," and "heat treatment" are not only indispensable but also inseparable.

You achieve the highest cutting performance when all work together; otherwise, you may compromise the others to compensate for one.

Steel Selection

The key to proper steel selection is twofold. The first step involves matching the alloy's inherent properties, bestowed by its chemistry, to the knife's intended use. The second is to match the alloy's complexity with the maker's approach to working it.

Some steels possess properties that make them better suited for certain blade types. From tough-

Even a tuna can lid can be sharpened to cut paper, but little more without proper steel or heat treatment.

switching to alloys that respond well to more traditional methods in a forge.

When the steel is poorly selected, you will subsequently see altered geometries and heat treatments to compensate. For a long time, the steel industry has been at it, developing proven methods of treating each alloy to its full potential for applications much more critical than a humble knife blade.

When knifemakers find themselves resorting to procedures that would have a professional heat treater scratching their head with a raised eyebrow, it can be a clear sign of an alloy not suited for the task or methods. It is no coincidence that so many of these heat treatments often involve rather rudimentary heat sources with alloyed steels, while every knifemaker using a well-controlled oven simply heat treats the alloys like everybody else.

Don't get too hung up on marketing that touts fad super steels or alloys. The truth of the matter is that steel selection is still only one-third of the equation. If you don't give the other two parts equal consideration, the greatest steel ever made will only be a sales gimmick. While there are some fine new alloys, classic steels have the advantage of having been around long enough for makers to have

ness for chopping to abrasion resistance in finer cuts, there are alloy chemistries to do each job. Choosing the wrong steel may result in compromises and a lot of extra effort to force it to do something for which its designer did not intend.

The second point considers the maker's ability to work the chosen steel. Whether it is a maker experienced with a forge or one with a digitally controlled oven, both can give you an excellent blade if they choose the correct steel for their approach. Similarly, either one might disappoint if they work outside of their comfort zone.

When my "high tech" heat treating equipment was recently offline for some long-needed updates, I continued to provide the same level of quality in my knives simply by

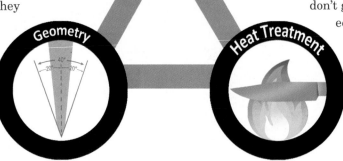

Edged excellence is the result of three critical factors the maker must master.

mastered using them in the complete package.

Ask the maker why they chose the steel for that blade. Listen for well-considered reasons why the properties of the alloy work best for that knife. Make a note of any indications of cutting corners. Quality steel is perhaps the least expensive part of a knife. If a maker sounds like they cheap out on it, compare it to what they are charging you and let that sink in.

Geometry

Of the three parts of our triangle, geometry may be the most overlooked. Geometry covers everything from handle shapes to blade profiles, but I will confine this conversation to the basic trigonometry of edges for the sake of this article.

Demonstrations of cutting ability typically display either good or bad geometry, revealing very little about the chosen alloy or its heat treatment. I would feel cheated by the flea market vendor of imported cutlery who did not fillet some paper for me. My son got an imported chef's knife for Christmas this year, and to demonstrate the absurdity of paper cutting, I threw a sheet of typing paper in the air to cleanly slice it in half before showing him how to sharpen that knife.

And, of course, for demonstrating that razor-like edge, there is shaving hair. Once again, it seems impressive, but a blade only needs to be so sharp to show that knifemakers suffer from mange on their arms. Sadly, the ability to slice paper or shave hair is a cut above the sharpness level of too many knives makers sell today. But the problem is that quick demonstrations of sharpness only show that any metal can have a sharp edge put on it. A tuna can lid may be sharpened to the level of many knives, but a quality cutting tool results from well-chosen steel with a heat treatment to support that edge in *repeated* use.

And, finally, there is an outright abuse of knives in misguided attempts to show quality while proving quite the opposite. An overzealous maker hacking and stabbing at materials you have never considered taking a knife to is mostly demonstrating how miserable that object will be to use as a knife due to absurd geometries required to handle the abuse.

Look at the edge geometry of any steel cutting or masonry tool and ask yourself if you would want to slice a tomato or skin game with it. You will be doing yourself, and the knifemaking community, a service by not encouraging this sort of marketing.

This caution is not to say that there are no genres of knives made for rugged use. Repairs I have made to military knives clearly show that warfighters do not use them lightly. But all my friends who make honest knives for demanding outdoor use sell them as such and do not try to convince you that they are razors or scissors.

Sorting Good from Bad

Fortunately, it can be relatively easy to sort good from bad in edge geometries, often just with a glance. Where the rubber hits the road in cutting is the facet created by sharpening what knifemakers refer to as the "secondary bevel." The narrower this polished line is, the more refined the geometry. Wide secondary bevels indicate an awkwardly thick grind.

Different knife applications call for various edge geometries within a range from a 22-degree blade bevel for heavy use to lower than 12 degrees for fine cuts. I learned this lesson the hard way by making an 18-degree edge angle for chefs who preferred less than 14 degrees.

One method to assess

Through his excellent text *Messerklingen und Stahl*, Roman Landes wrote the book on knife edges. There is no doubt his blades will cut.

this angle is to place the sharpened blade flat on a smooth piece of hardwood and then begin to lift the spine while pushing the edge over the wood. The point at which the edge first bites is the sharpening angle for the knife. If the angle, measured from the wood surface to the center of the blade spine, is greater than 22 degrees, the included angle (the

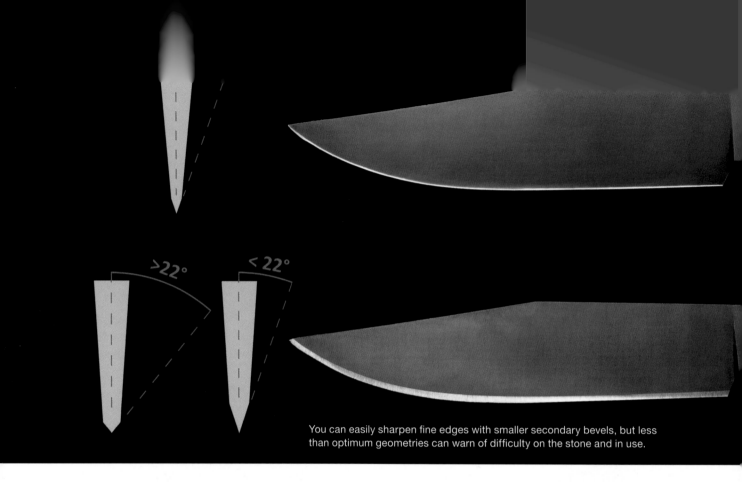

You can easily sharpen fine edges with smaller secondary bevels, but less than optimum geometries can warn of difficulty on the stone and in use.

sum of both sides) will be approaching 45 degrees and beyond what is desirable for cutting and sharpening.

To sharpen such an edge at a lower angle, you will have to wear away a lot of steel before engaging the actual cutting interface, resulting in the wide secondary angle and a lot of effort in sharpening. The wide secondary bevel will become challenging to sharpen after a couple of trips to the stone. The thick edge, sharpened at high angles, will not cut well and be terrible to sharpen right out of the box.

An overly thick grind is often a case of geometry compensating for heat treatment. When a maker speaks of ease of sharpening in terms of blade hardness, it is a warning sign that they may not understand these geometry concepts. Hard abrasives designed for sharpening are more than a match for any steel, and there are always diamond hones.

Now I am no slouch at making steel hard, but not that good! Every case I have encountered of a knife being difficult to sharpen has been a matter of geometry that, after reshaping, needs only a few strokes on the stone regardless of the hardness level. Modern steel alloys have high abrasion resistance due to carbide volumes, but isn't that the point? The trait that makes you take a few more strokes on the stone is the same quality that allows

you to take dozens of more cuts in use. Handicapping such steel by softening it rather than correcting the geometry will only give you a blunt edge that will quickly get worse.

Heat Treatment

A carefully chosen steel, shaped ideally to perform a task, requires a heat treatment designed for both. Some makers will be eager to tell you all about their heat treatment; if not, you should feel free to ask. But, in either case, knowing what to listen for will allow you to hear much more than you or they may realize.

The intangible nature of heat treatment can make it seem much more impressive or intimidating than it is. A knifemaker who gets too metaphysical as they struggle to communicate something rooted in fundamental physics and chemistry might not really get it or think that you won't. On the other hand, I have noticed a recent trend of armchair metallurgy among knifemakers, for which I may be partially responsible.

So, let's get it out of the way—I am sorry! A proper understanding of steel is more than quoting a few impressive words. The quickest way to sort out a pretender is to ask them to explain it in layman's terms and observe how effortlessly they switch gears or how much they grind them while struggling with the clutch.

A little common sense goes a long way here. A knifemaker selling you on "patented allotropic crystalline conversion process" is saying, "Put your wallet away and run!" Rest assured that if they came up with something that impressive, they would not be at a local knife show trying to make ends meet with blades they ground in their garage.

Rockwell numbers are often used to imply the excellence of a blade but are just a quality control tool for the heat treatment process. Rockwell numbers have no meaning by themselves since ideal hardness is entirely relative to, you guessed it, steel selection and geometry.

Identical Rockwell numbers will give you different results depending on the alloy. You could prop up an utterly inadequate hardness by reshaping the edge at the expense of cutting efficiency. Remembering that marketing is all about the person making the sales pitch, if Rockwell numbers tell you nothing about the knife, they may indicate that the maker cares enough about their process to do the testing.

Proper heat treatment results from a deep understanding of steel carefully chosen for our methods, not how much money we spend on equipment. I work with some sophisticated gadgets in my shop, and I can tell you that, without hard-earned skills and knowledge, all they can do is allow you to make a lousy knife more quickly.

An excellent maker will be able to give you a great knife using any equipment, but he may sacrifice time efficiency without his preferred tools. A new maker who relies on buying fancy equipment as a replacement for experience is, at best, giving you the same thing as a factory, except the industrial pros know how to use those tools.

How long has the maker been crafting and using knives? Do they understand the relationship between choosing the correct steel for the job, shaping the tool to do the job, and heat-treating that tool to excel at that job? Does the knife do what its designer intended? Beyond this, all you have is more marketing. □

While invaluable for checking heat treatment, Rockwell testing sheds little light on other aspects of knife performance.

BLADE®
Adds ICCE to Knife Show Lineup

The Caribou Media acquisition is a strategic complement to the BLADE Show.

By Mike Haskew

n the fall of 2020, Caribou Media Group, LLC stepped up its commitment to expand in the sphere of custom knives.

The International Custom Cutlery Exhibition (ICCE) acquisition furthers the company's contribution to the industry through the colossus that is the annual BLADE Show and its signature event in California, BLADE Show West. The addition is bound to support the growth of custom knives just as a rising tide lifts all boats, and frankly, the time had come for ICCE to essentially "graduate."

The successor to the original Knifemakers' Guild Show, ICCE made its first appearance in Kansas City, Missouri, in 2015 and moved to Fort Worth, Texas, with its March 2019 event. Through it all, ICCE has featured top-of-the-line knives of Guild and American Bladesmith Society (ABS) exhibitors.

Under the leadership of custom knifemaker Jerry Moen and others, the show matured. It now offers a venue for the best makers in the business and knife aficionados to mingle, exchange information, and generally promote one another.

The ICCE came about through a working partnership between The Knifemakers' Guild and ABS. Featuring exhibitors from the Guild and ABS exclusively, the ICCE, as initially conceived, filled a valuable niche in the market as it developed in Kansas City and then at the Fort Worth Stockyards National Historic District.

First announced in the autumn of 2020, the acquisition of ICCE by Caribou Media and BLADE Show generated quite a buzz. The rationale for the process to be completed was apparent to everyone involved. Moen, who served as executive director for the independent ICCE, saw an opportunity when BLADE Show executives expressed interest in acquiring the event to add to their robust calendar.

"I put on seven of these shows, and Harvey Dean and I have been responsible for it coming together," reflected Moen. "Having the show in Texas has been great because of oil and cattle money and people who love knives here. It has really been magical."

At age 71, Moen recognized that the level of involvement required for the ICCE to continue to grow and prosper would be better served with the group of professionals from Caribou Media that make the annual BLADE Show such a recurring and resonating success.

Future Health of ICCE

Moen consulted with Dean, a legendary master bladesmith and ABS board member since 2004, and with Knifemakers' Guild President Gene Baskett. The decision to work with Caribou Media and the BLADE Show was perceived as a proper course of action for the future health of the ICCE.

"I talked with both Gene and Harvey, and they said working with BLADE was a great idea. The show is more than just selling knives; it's also about being there," Moen commented. "I always thought it would be the answer to the worldwide presence of the Guild and the ABS, and today the only way ICCE can do what it needs is through the help of BLADE Show management."

Timing is everything, and when Henry Wu, group chief executive officer of Caribou's Gun Digest Media, and BLADE Show Director Alicia Newton reached out, the dialogue rolled along at a steady pace.

"When Henry and Alicia called and asked if we

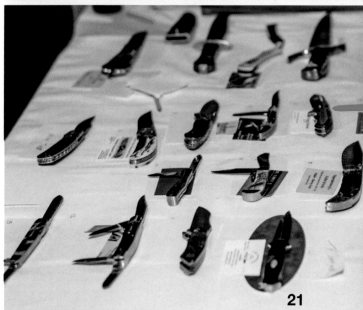

Attendees and exhibitors interact on the floor of the 2019 BLADE Show in Atlanta. The annual event is always much anticipated, and the ICCE, now under BLADE Show management, delivers the same kind of excitement.

a consultant. He is doing so with the full support of Dean and Baskett.

"Jerry talked to me, and we agreed that the BLADE folks would do a good job," Dean noted. "They will be effective in getting the word out, and the potential is there for it to be great with the Fort Worth Stockyards location and knives fitting right in there as they do. We were all ready to go with them, and Jerry and I put a lot of effort into the ICCE through those earlier years."

Baskett joined in, "The Guild Board is pleased with the progress after the acquisition and glad that BLADE Show is taking over to make ICCE one of the premier shows in the industry."

Turning it Loose

"We believed that, as soon as the COVID pandemic subsided, people would want to get out and spend their money, and we know that the BLADE

were interested in doing a deal, I told Henry that I wanted to keep it high quality because high-quality knifemakers bring high-quality buyers in the door and help us sell product, meet people and learn new things," Moen explained. "If you don't sell knives, then exhibitors aren't interested in coming back."

The one-two punch of BLADE Show expertise and ICCE star power debuted at the Fort Worth Stockyards in March 2021.

"The company is always looking for new opportunities to expand the BLADE brand name," Newton related. "We have a high concentration of makers and subscribers in the Texas area. Therefore, taking over the show in Texas was a natural fit. We definitely feel it is a location that offers great growth potential and has become a mainstay in the knife community."

Moen, a voting member of the Guild who has served several years on the organization's board of directors, agreed to stay on with the ICCE for three years to facilitate the transition and serve as

Jerry Moen (left) presents the award for Best Fixed Blade to Josh Fisher during the 2019 ICCE event.
(Scott Schuster Photography)

The legendary Harvey Dean (left) stands with custom knifemakers J.W. Randall (center) and Shayne Carter (right) during the 2019 ICCE. *(Scott Schuster Photography)*

Show folks want to make ICCE a premier custom knife show," Baskett remarked. "We are looking forward to the future, and we know the BLADE Show has the expertise to turn this thing loose. A lot of the custom knifemakers are pleased with it too."

Moen remained with the new ICCE and its BLADE Show shepherds because he understands the critical need for a liaison. "I'm staying because I know the show politics around here," he reasoned. "I'll stick with it as long as I can, anything to make it work. We decided to make this change because it needed to be done. I have been a one-man show, and I can't grow the ICCE like it should be grown on my own."

"Prior to the change, we had had two consecutive sellout shows," he continued, "so I think the show will stay in Fort Worth for the near future. In the early stage of the transition, we went over, and I got the BLADE folks introduced to the people at the buildings and at the hotels and turned the keys over to them, so to speak. Alicia has done a marvelous job following along the same lines and will do a better job in the years to come than I did. I had a hard time keeping up with all the paperwork!"

Newton continues to manage the BLADE Show in Atlanta along with the revived BLADE Show West, and with the ICCE now on her plate, she expects the opportunity to soar. "We just don't want to come in right out of the gate and change everything," she related at the time of the acquisition while pledging that the venue would be exciting and complementary of everything that goes into the formula for a great knife event.

"In addition to the outstanding craftsmanship attendees can expect to find from our knife community, we will also be introducing products by high-end cowboy artisans," Newton said. "We believe these products will add a new element to the knife show and help distinguish it from other events in the community."

She continued, "This event won't be just another typical knife show but will have unique elements specific to Texas that will help set it apart. As noted, we will have about 20 to 25 high-end cowboy artisans that will be displaying and selling their

Above: The BLADE Show floor is abuzz with excitement during the 2019 event.

Left: An exchange of information occurs right on the custom knifemaker's table during the 2019 ICCE in Fort Worth, Texas. BLADE Show management has acquired the ICCE and will coordinate future shows. *(Scott Schuster Photography)*

products at the event."

"In addition, as the show continues to grow," Newton proposes, "we will introduce experiences specific to the Texas show that won't take place at our other BLADE Show events. Finally, the weekend will be fully immersive in that, when the show is over, attendees can take in all the sights and sounds of the Fort Worth area without even having to get into a car."

Without question, the communication powerhouse of the BLADE Show's promotional resources, specifically the internet, live events, and the staunchly loyal subscription base of BLADE Magazine, are keys to the future promotional effort of the new ICCE.

Grassroots Marketing

Newton added, "In the immediate future, there are no plans to add staff positions. However, the show will be promoted through our magazine and social media assets as well as through an extensive local grassroots marketing campaign and partnerships with local businesses."

High hopes characterize the future of the BLADE Show production of ICCE. Moen, probably the individual who has invested the most significant amount of time and effort in the event, is optimistic.

"I believe with all my heart that the ICCE will be an even more quality event and a world-class show when nurtured properly," he offered. "It will become one of BLADE's stars. We had probably 1,500 visitors in 2019 and did little advertising with a few VIP passes. We could have had twice that much, but the sellout was at 125 tables. It was a small show, but the best of the best was there, and I know you cannot limit a show to that. To make a show really expand and grow as it should, you have to accept new people."

Some say that a firm foundation is a basis for a sound structure, something of lasting value, and the organizers and original proponents of the ICCE put that foundation in place.

Moen reflects on his time in the Guild and those early shows in Orlando, Florida. Simply put, they meant a lot to him, fostering camaraderie and helping him set his sights on the excellence that he sought from the beginning of his custom knifemaking career.

The late, great Tony Bose once said that the ICCE was "the best start-up show" that he had ever seen—high praise for those who devoted themselves to the effort despite difficulties that sometimes arise in any endeavor.

When Moen refers to those early shows as "magical," he means it. Nothing, it seems, would give him more pleasure than to know that a young person's interest in custom knives has been kindled and then elevated through communication, dialogue, sharing of tips and pointers, and genuine interest that cannot be found anywhere else like on the floor of a well-managed, attended and executed knife show.

Now, the BLADE Show and its long tradition of excellence have taken the leading role in the future development of ICCE. It will join a network of renowned knife events that now stretches from the East with the show in Atlanta to the California coast via BLADE Show West and stopping off in the country's center through an ICCE spectacular in Fort Worth.

Time will tell whether the convergence of all these resources and the expertise available will generate the desired results. Still, the legacy and roots of those involved are too deep and rich to produce anything but a resounding triumph. And all is for the betterment of the custom knife industry. □

A good crowd attends the proceedings held during dinner at a steakhouse on the grounds of the Fort Worth Stockyards during the 2019 ICCE. *(Scott Schuster Photography)*

HISTORY OF U.S. KNIFE LAWS

The author delves into little-known historic knife ordinances and restrictions.

By Evan F. Nappen, Attorney at Law

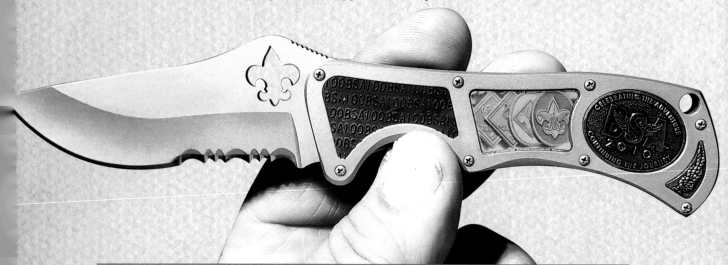

Unlike a 1644–1657 Massachusetts Bay Colony law that required 10- to 16-year-olds to train with half pikes and other arms, U.S. schools today have "zero intelligence" policies for any knife, be it a Boy Scout pocketknife (shown), Swiss Army Knife or plastic birthday cake cutter. The Boy Scout 100th Anniversary Commemorative Knife features a fleur-de-lis cut-out, and the handle has a hologram insert with Tenderfoot, Webelos, Wolf, and Bear emblems. The Northwest Territorial Mint made the knife for the Boy Scouts of America.

Knife laws have existed on U.S. soil since before the Pilgrims landed at Plymouth Rock in 1620. The earliest known knife law in North America is a Virginia Colony ordinance from 1619 that mandated persons bring their *"Swordes"* (swords) and other arms to *"divine service and sermons:"*

All persons whatsoever upon the Saboath days shall frequent divine service and sermons both forenoon and afternoon; and shall bring their pieces, Swordes, powder and shot.

This law contrasts with modern times where many states prohibit personal defense weapons in houses of worship, and when nowhere in the United States are people required under the law to bring weapons to church or temple.

Given the rash of attacks on churches, synagogues, and mosques, some states have passed legislation permitting attendees to be armed.

In 1642, New York had one of the first criminal laws restricting knife use. The "Ordinance of the Director and Council of New Netherland Against Drawing a Knife and Inflicting a Wound Therewith" proclaimed:

. . . No one shall presume to draw a knife much less to would any person, under the penalty of fl.50, to be paid immediately, or, in default, to work three months with the Negroes in chains; this, without any respect of person. Let everyone take heed against damage and be warned.

The penalty for violation was a punishment of three months forced labor "with the Negroes in chains." The humiliation factor of this sentence for a white colonist must have been a deterrent. This New York law shows the cruel racism towards blacks, even in 1642.

New Jersey's attitude toward knives and other edged weapons has not changed much from its Colonial days and has even gotten worse. The Province of New Jersey, in 1686, had "An Act Against Wearing Swords, etc." that proclaimed:

Whereas there hath been great complaint by the inhabitants of this Province, that several persons wearing swords, daggers, pistols, dirks, stilettoes, skeines, or any other unusual or unlawful weapons. . . And be it further enacted by the authority aforesaid, that no person or persons after publication hereof, shall presume privately to wear any pocket pistol, skeines, stilettoes, daggers or dirks, or other unusual or unlawful weapons within this Province, ...And ...that no planter shall ride or go armed with sword, pistol or dagger, upon the penalty of five pounds, to be levied as aforesaid, excepting all officers, civil and military, and soldiers while in actual service, as also all strangers, travelling upon their lawful occasions through this Province, behaving themselves peaceably.

"Skeines" refers to the famous Scottish dirk known as a sgian-dubh (a hidden "black" knife worn in the stock-

The Randall Arkansas Toothpick Model 13 came with a Roughback Johnson sheath, an Ivorite handle, and brass hilt and butt. It is a traditional toothpick pattern from the 1800s. In 1838, Arkansas created "An Act to Suppress the Sale and Use of Bowie Knives and Arkansas Tooth Picks in this State."

ing or boot).

Today, in New Jersey, possessing "*skeines, stilettoes, daggers or dirks,*" even in one's home, is a felony-level offense carrying a maximum sentence of 18 months in state prison; and contemporary New Jersey has no "*...travelling upon their lawful occasions through this Province, behaving themselves peaceably*" or "*peaceable journey*" exemption to the law.

In fact, in New Jersey, preemptively arming oneself for self-defense outside one's home is unlawful with any weapon, including a pocketknife, sheath knife, ax, machete, sword, martial arts weapon, or kitchen knife.

From 1644-1657, the Massachusetts Bay Colony enacted the following law requiring 10- to 16-year-olds to train with half pikes and other arms:

Whereas it is conceived that ye training up of youth to ye art and practice of armes will be of great use to this country...it is therefore ordered all youth within this jurisdiction, from ten years old to ye age of 16 years, shall be instructed ...

The rare Hall Breechloading Rifle Bayonet of 1819 is one of the first 100 bayonets made by Simon North and marked "US/SN." North shipped it to Harper's Ferry for inspection.

in ye exercise of armes, as small guns, half pikes, bows and arrows...

Imagine if such training were required of modern youth. Instead, U.S. schools today have "zero intelligence" policies for any knife, be it a Boy Scout pocketknife, Swiss Army Knife, or plastic birthday cake cutter.

Yet, our teachers could be teaching our children knife safety as, for decades, the Boy Scouts of America (BSA) has taught Scouts how to safely handle knives, saws, and axes via the BSA's Totin' Chip Card. The card "grants Scouts the right to carry and use woods tools" after they have demonstrated "proper handling, care and use of the pocketknife, ax and saw."

Government taking knives and other arms from people is nothing new. It often bases such abuse on political considerations. In 1779, Pennsylvania passed "An Act ... for Disarming Persons Who Shall Not Have Given Attestations of Allegiance and Fidelity to this State." The law mandated:

...the lieutenant or any sub lieutenant of the militia of any county or place within this state, shall be, and is hereby empowered to disarm any person or persons ... suspected to be disaffected to the independence of this state, and shall take from every such person any cannon, mortar, or other piece of ordinance, or any blunderbuss, wall piece, musket, fusee, carbine or pistols, or other fire arms, or any hand gun; and any sword, cutlass, bayonet, pike or other warlike weapon, out of any building, house or place belonging to such person.

This law, however, was enacted during the American Revolutionary War, and during wartime, governments often curtail civil rights. State militia laws enacted before, during, and after the Revolution frequently contained requirements regarding edged weapons.

One of the most significant Second Amendment state court opinions concerning knives is 1984's Oregon Supreme Court Case of *State v. Delgado*. The Delgado Court found that switchblades were protected by Oregon's State Constitutional Right to Keep and Bear Arms. In the decision, the court gives a history of knives as "arms" and points out the laws at the time, which required militiamen to carry "jackknives:"

Even when they joined the American Army during the revolution, the knife they carried was the jackknife, which was mentioned frequently in colonial records. During the American Revolution at least two states, New Hampshire and New York, required their militiamen to carry a jackknife. Even during the mid-18th century, some of these "jackknives" were rather more lethal than their name suggests, measuring two feet long with the blade extended, and designed solely for fighting.

In the landmark *D.C. v. Heller*, the 2008 U.S. Supreme Court held that the Second Amendment confirmed fundamental, individual rights. Writing for the majority opinion, Justice Antonin Scalia quoted the Kessler case of the Oregon Supreme Court. The court cited Kessler in the above Delgado switchblade case. In his citing Kessler, Scalia referenced the late George Neumann, whose book helped the court to clarify that "arms" includes knives:

In the colonial and Revolutionary War era, [small-arms] weapons used by militiamen and weapons used in defense of person and home were one and the same." *State v. Kessler, 289 Ore. 359, 368, 614 P. 2d 94, 98 (1980) (citing G. Neumann, Swords and Blades of the American Revolution 6–15, 252–254 (1973)).*

Some examples of early state militia laws that mandated edged weapons include:

Virginia, 1757: "An Act for Better Regulating and Disciplining the Militia"

WHEREAS it is necessary, in this time of danger, that the militia of this Colony should be well regulated and disciplined … that every person so as aforesaid enlisted (except free mulattoes, negroes, and Indians) shall be armed in the manner following, that is to say: Every soldier shall be furnished with a firelock well fixed, a bayonet fitted to the same, a double cartouche box …

Vermont, 1779: "An Act for Forming and Regulating the Militia"

That every listed soldier and other householder shall always be provided with, and have in constant readiness, a well-fixed firelock … or other good firearms … a good sword, cutlass, tomahawk or bayonet; a worm, and priming wire, fit for each gun; a cartouche box or powder and bullet pouch; one pound of good powder, four pounds of bullets for his gun, and six good flints….

Missouri, 1818: Militia

Each militia man shall provide

The Swiss Army Climber Knife is a 125th Anniversary Special Edition from the Evan Nappen collection.

himself with-in one month from the date of his enrollment with a good musket, a sufficient bayonet and belt, or a fusil, two spare flints, a knapsack and pouch with a box there-in to contain twenty-four cartridges suited …

We also find regulations concerning edged weapons in laws prohibiting dueling. In one of the earliest, 1719, Massachusetts passed "An Act for the Punishing and Preventing of Dueling." At a time when men took honor seriously, dueling with edged weapons was a genuine concern. The law stated:

… That whoever … fight a duel, combat, or engage in a rencounter with rapier, or small-sword, back-sword, pistol, or any other dangerous weapon, to the danger of life, mayhem, or wounding of the parties, or the affray of his Majesty's good subjects (although death doth not thereby ensue) and be thereof convicted, by due course of law, before the Court of Assize, or Court of General Sessions of the Peace, in the respective Counties of this Province, shall be punished by fine, not exceeding a

One of the most significant Second Amendment state court opinions concerning knives is 1984's Oregon Supreme Court case of *State v. Delgado*. The Delgado Court found that switchblades were protected by Oregon's State Constitutional Right to Keep and Bear Arms. The Pat Havlin picklock switchblade shown here is a traditional Italian pattern with stag handle scales.

hundred pounds, imprisonment, not exceeding six months, or corporally punished ...

This penalty not only included a potentially high fine and imprisonment but also "corporal" punishment, which meant flogging or other forms of physical abuse. However, although Massachusetts wanted to discourage dueling, it realized that sometimes gentlemen had to do what honor demanded and that punishment could also be simply a hefty fine.

After that, several states regulated blades and dueling. Pennsylvania's Act is one of the earliest, and Louisiana and Mississippi enacted their anti-dueling laws after the infamous 1827 Sandbar Fight that made James Bowie and his knife a legend.

Pennsylvania, 1779: "An Act for the Suppression of Vice and Immorality"

That if any person within this commonwealth shall challenge the person of another to fight at sword, pistol, rapier or other dangerous weapon, such person so challenging shall forfeit and pay for every such offense (being lawfully convicted by the testimony of one or more credible witnesses, or by the confession of the party offending,) the sum of five hundred pounds, or suffer twelve months imprisonment without bail or mainprise ...

Louisiana, 1828: "Crimes"

If any person shall challenge another, or shall accept a challenge to fight with sword, pistol, rapier or other dangerous weapon, every person so challenging or accepting such challenge, shall, upon conviction thereof, be fined not exceeding five hundred dollars, and may be imprisoned not exceeding two years.

Mississippi, 1838: "An Act to Prevent the Evil Practice of Dueling in this State"

... if any person or persons shall be guilty of fighting in any corporate city or town, or any other town, or public place, in this state, and shall in such fight use any rifle, shot gun, sword,

sword cane, pistol, dirk, bowie knife, dirk knife, or any other deadly weapon; ... shall be fined not less than three hundred dollars, and shall be imprisoned not less than three months; and if any person shall be killed in such fight, the person so killing the other may also be prosecuted and convicted as in other cases of murder.

The fear and notoriety of the bowie knife convinced some states to focus on the knife itself and not the person misusing it. These states banned carrying bowie knives.

Arkansas, 1838: "An Act to Suppress the Sale and Use of Bowie Knives and Arkansas Tooth Picks in this State"

That if any person shall wear any Bowie knife, Arkansas tooth pick, or other knife or weapon that shall in form, shape or size resemble a Bowie knife or Arkansas toothpick under his clothes, or keep the same concealed about his person, such person shall be guilty of a misdemeanor.

Racism and anti-weapon laws often go hand in hand. In 1807, federal law prohibited supplying weapons to Indians, including *"knives, spears, battle aces, tome-hawks."* It was known as the "Act to Prevent the Disposing of Arms, and Other Warlike Implements, and Ammunition to Indians and Others, in Laws of the Indiana Territory," and mandated:

... any person or persons, who shall directly or indirectly, by gift, present, donation, loan, sale or otherwise furnish and provide, or have furnished and provided any Indian or Indians, with ... deadly weapons, such as knives, spears, battle axes, tome-hawks,

This commemorative bowie knife duplicates the known Rezin Bowie pattern. Louisiana and Mississippi enacted their 1828 and 1838 anti-dueling laws after the infamous 1827 Sandbar Fight that made James Bowie and his knife a legend.

Today, in New Jersey, possessing *"skeines, stilettoes, daggers or dirks,"* even in one's home, is a felony-level offense carrying a maximum sentence of 18 months in state prison. "Skeines" refers to the famous Scottish dirks known as sgian-dubhs. The vintage Black Watch Royal Highlanders Regimental silver-mounted sgian-dubh has a Scottish fly plaid brooch.

before the Civil War, North Carolina had such a law in 1840 requiring Blacks to obtain a license before being allowed to possess knives:

That if any free negro, mulatto, or free person of color, shall wear or carry about his or her person, or keep in his or her house, any shot gun, musket, rifle, pistol, sword, dagger or bowie-knife, unless he or she shall have obtained a license therefor from the Court of Pleas and Quarter Sessions of his or her county, within one year preceding the wearing, keeping or carrying thereof, he or she shall be guilty of a misdemeanor ...

In Texas, people have been prohibited from possession of bowie knives, daggers, dirks, and other knives by way of 150-year-old laws. These statutes focused enforcement on Hispanics to counter the Tejano "blade culture." It was not until 2017, thanks in large part to the efforts of Knife Rights, Inc., that activists finally reformed these Texas knife laws.

We can learn from our history. We must fight to repeal or reform any knife laws that promote racism, do nothing to stop actual crime, or turn honest knife owners into criminals. Thus, the battle for knife liberty continues across America.

Special thanks to the Repository of Historical Gun Laws, Duke University School of Law, *https://firearmslaw.duke.edu/*, a priceless resource for this article. □

pistols [susils, rifles, smooth bores, or muskets] ... shall, upon conviction by indictment ... be fined in any sum not exceeding one thousand dollars, be whipped publickly [sic], any number of stripes, not exceeding one hundred well laid on, and be imprisoned for a term not exceeding five years ...

Modern-day federal knife laws still prohibit the possession of switchblades, gravity knives, and ballistic knives in "Indian Country," even though possession of these knives is not banned in the states by federal law.

Of course, it was not just Indians who were denied their Constitutional Right to Keep and Bear Arms by anti-knife laws. After the Civil War, southern state "Black Codes" prohibited Blacks from possessing knives or other weapons. Even

SHARPENING STRAIGHT RAZORS

There is nothing like a nice, smooth straight razor shave using a keen blade.

By Tim Zowada

Straight razor shaving continues to grow in popularity. An ever-increasing crowd has discovered using a traditional straight razor is the ultimate in shaving closeness and comfort. Sadly, many potential devotees have given up on straight razors. This situation is usually due to poor honing, shave technique, or both. To help rectify the problem, we will discuss the basic concepts of razor honing.

The first thing to consider is whether the razor is worth honing. These days, there a lot of junk razors on the market. That includes new and used razors. There are a plethora of imported razors that have horrible steel, heat treatment, and geometry. Fortunately, it is not difficult to spot crummy razors.

It is best to stick with newly manufactured razors from known companies or classic razors from reputable sources. It is always wise to seek the advice of those with experience. If lacking a knowledgeable mentor, there are a few things to look for.

The spine thickness, relative to the width of the razor, is extremely important. The spine or back of the blade is the honing angle guide for all stone and strop work. Looking at the blade from the end, imagine a triangle formed between the cutting edge and both sides of the spine.

This triangle should have an included angle of 15-18 degrees at the cutting edge. If it is less than 15 degrees, the edge will tend to wrinkle or chip. Greater than 18 degrees will lead to difficulty in honing and shaving. For those who do not love trigonometry, the width of the blade should be roughly 3-4 times the thickness of the spine.

Left: This old razor shows most of the problems inherent in improper honing and care. The honing bevel is wide and uneven, and there is excessive hone wear on the spine.

The profile of the edge is also important. The edge, viewed from the side, should be either straight or slightly convex. It is easy to see this by gently putting the blade edge down on a flat surface and shining a light from the opposite side. If the edge touches the flat surface at more than one point, it is concave and needs repair. Be aware, do not perform this test with a freshly honed razor. It will dull the edge. Still, it is an excellent way to check a razor before purchase.

The honing bevel will give several clues about the quality of the razor — the blade area that touches the stone and strop during maintenance. Ideally, the honing angle should be narrow, even in width, and identical on both sides of the razor. A wide honing bevel creates more work in honing and stropping. There is more metal to remove than with a narrow bevel.

Do not be fooled by some Damascus steel razors that appear to have wide honing bevels. Many Damascus razors have an area that is not etched near the edge, giving the false impression of a wide honing bevel. An uneven honing bevel shows either improper sharpening, an edge that is not straight, or overall poor grinding.

Sharpening Stones

Sharpening stones, otherwise known as hones, form the basis of a razor-sharpening system. Generally, you hone razors using water stones. These stones use water as a lubricant rather than oil. Many of these stones are the same as those used for sharpening knives, planes, and chisels. The big difference lies in the grits used. While you use a 4,000-grit stone as the final finishing step on a knife, it is often a good starting point for honing razors.

When starting, begin with less expensive stones. As abilities and preferences grow over time, it is easy to spend a lot of money. Technique and understanding go a lot further toward producing a good edge than do expensive stones. The costly stones make the job a little easier.

Brands to look for include Norton, Naniwa, Shapton, and King. To start, 4,000- and 8,000-grit stones are sufficient. If there will be minor edge repair, a 1,000-grit water stone or diamond plate can be handy.

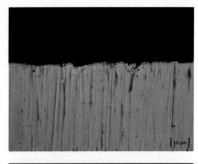

After honing on a Norton 4,000-grit waterstone, the edge is jagged and uneven. Yet, this would be an excellent edge for a knife. The honing bevel ends at the bottom of the frame and is less than 50µ or .00002 inches wide. For comparison, a piece of typing paper is about 100µ thick.

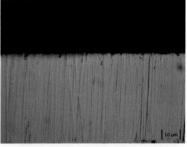

After honing with a Norton 8,000-grit waterstone, the edge is smoothed considerably and slightly rounded.

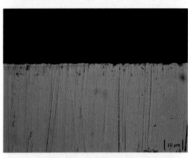

A vintage Escher finishing stone flattens the edge and refines the honing angle.

The effect of using a canvas hanging strop is subtle, as it burnishes and straightens the edge. Overuse of a canvas strop can damage the edge.

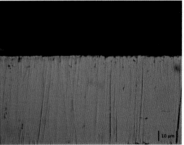

The horsehide hanging strop was employed to polish the edge.

A micrograph image of a chin whisker for size reference.

The finishing stones are where fables and delusions of grandeur enter. The finishing stone is the last in the honing progression before moving on to strops. They are usually in the 12,000- to the 16,000-grit range. There is much debate on what is the best "finisher." An important concept to remember is that the purpose of stonework is to set you up for good stropping.

A good place to start is with a Naniwa or Shapton 12,000-grit stone. In the future, it is wonderful to play with the classic natural finishing stones. Escher, Coticule, Translucent Arkansas, Japanese natural stones (Jnats), and more all beckon to those who cannot simply leave well enough alone.

With all the stones, be careful when shopping. Price is not always indicative of quality!

Lapping the Stones

No matter what stones you end up with, you should lap them. None of the available stones come ready for use out of the box. The purpose of lapping is twofold: first, to flatten the stone's surface, and second, to expose fresh abrasive.

The easiest way to start lapping is on a flat surface, using 400-grit silicon carbide sandpaper. The flat surface can be a granite surface plate, a thick piece of glass, or even a granite floor tile from a home improvement store. Clamp the sandpaper to the flat surface, wet the sandpaper with water, and rub the stone over the sandpaper surface.

Drawing a pencil grid on the surface of the stone will help show when the stone is flat. Pay special attention to avoid rocking the stone or putting pressure on one area. A figure-eight motion will help keep things under control.

Four hundred grit is sufficient for lapping the 4,000- and 8,000-grit stones. Yet, lapping higher

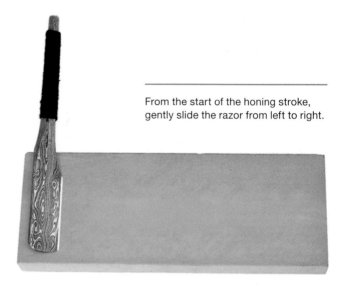

From the start of the honing stroke, gently slide the razor from left to right.

grit finishing stones will often be completed at 2,000 grit or higher. That's because the abrasive action of the sandpaper can leave scratches on the stone surfaces. These scratches change the effective grit of the stones and how they sharpen razors.

Once the stones are lapped flat, you should never have to flatten them again. All future lapping is to clean and refresh the surface of the stone. If the stone becomes "dished" during use and requires flattening, you've applied too much pressure to the razor. Or you've worked too long between refresh lapping. To always have fresh abrasive, some will lightly lap their stones before honing every razor.

There are other tools available for lapping. Most common are the 300-400-grit DMT Atoma and Shapton diamond lapping/sharpening plates. Still, silicon carbide sandpaper and a flat surface work just fine and could be all you ever need.

Final Stropping Step

Stropping is the final stage in sharpening a razor. While shaving immediately following the finishing stone hone is possible, the shave's smoothness, comfort, and closeness are improved by stropping.

Often, you'll use two or more strops after honing, before each shave. You can maintain a good razor for months before requiring a trip back to the hones if you've done the stropping well.

Most strops are made from either fabric or leather, with fabrics being various weaves of cotton or linen. Each fabric type imparts a unique character to the razor's edge. Some leather usually follows up the fabric strops. Leather types include various tannings of cow, horse, and even kangaroo! There are also vegan options available. Again, the different types of leather are unique in how

For honing and stropping, the razor lies flat with the spine and edge on the hone.

Notice that stropping is performed with the spine of the blade leading.

Back to the Stones

The assumption at this point is that the razor is in good shape and only needs re-sharpening. Razors that have chipped, blunt, or otherwise damaged edges will require more work on coarse stones.

The basis of honing is straightforward. The razor is laid flat on the stone, resting on both its spine and cutting edge. It is then slid, edge first, across a wet and properly lapped stone. At the stroke's end, roll the razor over its spine and stroke in the opposite direction. This movement is considered one "lap."

Assuming the razor does not need a lot of remedial work, the razor's weight is sufficient for downward pressure on the stone. Pushing the razor down on the stone only distorts the thin edge and can cause other problems. This concept is probably one of the most important and challenging to understand. Only the weight of the razor is needed!

Experienced honers use one hand to guide the blade across the stone, usually holding the razor near the junction of the blade and handle scales. The less adept, such as me, use both hands. If you use two hands, be sure the hand on the blade only guides it across the stone and does not push the edge down on the stone.

Several variations to this primary down and back stroke include the rolling stroke, X-stroke, and "circles," each for particular situations and blade shapes. You learn the techniques as each need arises and are all variations of the standard down and back stroke.

Smooth and Polish the Edge

Stropping is like stonework, with the functional differences being that strops are less abrasive, softer, and more flexible than stones. The goal is the same, to smooth and polish the edge of a razor.

Anchor the strop on one end, with most practitioners using a doorknob or fixture on a wall. Pull the other end tight, so the strop is taught and does not sag. Then, push and pull the blade from one end of the strop to the other. The difference from stonework is you push and pull the blade with the spine leading. Otherwise, you'll cut the strop.

Once again, to change direction, roll the blade over the spine. This method avoids damaging the

they affect the razor's edge and resulting shave.

Strop care is simple. Keep it clean and dry. When new, some of the coarse fabrics require softening. That's especially true of Kanayama canvas. A few cycles through the washing machine and using the bottom of a glass jar to rub the canvas will usually soften things up nicely.

Some people oil their leather strops, while others keep them clean and dry. Some go so far as to clean leather strops with rubbing alcohol. All are valid options and do affect how the strop works on a blade. There is plenty of room to experiment.

edge and cutting the strop.

Only use the weight of the razor. It is incredible, but the fabrics and leather are plenty abrasive and do not need pressure to be more effective. A good rule of thumb is that the blade should slide across the surface of the strop; you should not push it down into it.

Pushing down on the blade or allowing the strop to sag will significantly increase the honing angle at the cutting edge. You can easily see this effect when you take the blade back to the hone. If the edge has been dramatically rounded by stropping, the hone will not contact the razor's cutting edge. This situation calls for a lot of remedial work with coarse stones.

Stropping with a tight strop and no pressure does not alter the honing angle to a significant degree. Stropping does change things on a microscopic scale, but that is beyond the scope of this article.

Sample Honing Schedule
1. 4,000 grit – 20 laps
2. 8,000 grit – 20 laps
3. 12,000 grit – 20-30 laps
4. Coarse cotton or linen strop – 10 laps (It is surprising how aggressive these strops are!)
5. Finishing strop – 50 laps

Do all of these using the entire length of the

A close examination of the edge of Harvey Dean's classic damascus straight razor shows how applying a resistant substance such as nail polish helps protect the honing bevel from damage during blade etching. *(Francesco Pachi Photo)*

stone or with the strop. It is often helpful to perform five to 10 short, half-inch laps at the end of each step.

The Beard Test

The absolute best way to test a razor is to shave a beard. Nothing will give you better feedback on your honing. An adequately honed straight razor will shave smoothly, without pulling or irritation. While learning, other tests are helpful for feedback, but all of them have the potential to damage a well-honed razor.

The same goes for micrographs taken with a reflected-light microscope. They are useful for research and getting "pictures in your head," yet they do not tell you everything. With this type of microscope, you'll only see the honing bevel's side. Often an edge that looks great under the microscope will shave horribly. Use a scanning electron microscope to see what is going on clearly. Maybe someday…

Corrosion is the biggest enemy of a sharp razor. After honing and shaving, coat the razor with a rust preventative oil. Some favorites are Ballistol, mineral oil, and Camellia Oil. You can easily wipe these oils off before stropping.

It would be best if you stropped a straight razor before each shave. A typical routine is 10 laps on canvas or linen and 50 laps on leather. Once the

Kamisori-style razors were used for the micrographs. They sit better on the microscope than do western-style razors. Plus, they are lovely to shave with. The lack of handle scales allows for much better control while shaving.

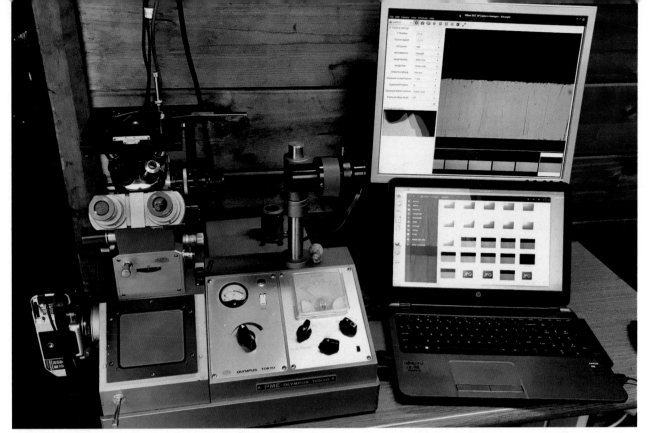

The author employed an Olympus microscope and imaging system for the blade edge photos herein.

strops no longer do the job, it is time for a trip back to the stones.

There are many ways to go about honing razors. The above is merely a starting point. Here are additional techniques and tools to consider:

1. Taping the spine before honing. The tape protects the spine of the blade from hone wear. The most critical application is on Damascus steel and engraved razors. Kapton tape is only .002-inch thick. The change in the effective honing angle is negligible. Electrical tape is thicker at about .007 inch. Use multiple layers of electrical tape to increase honing angles and tinker with removing micro-serrations from edges.

2. You can use lapping film, diamond, and other abrasives as a replacement for stones.

3. Bench Strops: hard-backed strops of leather, wood, and fabric. These are employed with and without various abrasive compounds. They are most often used as an intermediate step between the stones and hanging strops. Chromium oxide and diamond are standard abrasives.

4. Leather and fabric hanging strops with various abrasive compounds.

5. Edge trailing strokes on stones used for microscopic burr management.

6. Japanese natural Stones (Jnats). These are natural stones quarried in Japan. There is an unending array of types, hardness ratings, and grits. No two are alike. This niche is an amazing branch of honing where the slurry stone (tomo) is just as important as the base stone. For the obsessive nerd, it is a fascinating world.

7. Other natural stones. The list here is endless. Pre-World War II Eschers, Belgian Coticules, Thuringian, and Arkansas stones are prominent. There are many others.

Hopefully, this article gives you an excellent place to start sharpening and stropping straight razors, thus enjoying smooth shaves for years to come. □

Links:

heirloomrazorstrop.com/ Tony Miller – Wonderful leather and fabric strops

sharpeningsupplies.com/ - Norton, Naniwa, Shapton, and Coticule stones

aframestokyo.com/ Jnats and Kanayama strops

etsy.com/shop/TomoNagura Kieth Johnson - Jnats, Coticules, strops and misc.

scienceofsharp.com/home/ Fantastic articles on the microscopic world of sharpening

facebook.com/groups/859903791016625/ user/704371670 Jonathan Coe – A one-man show. Various custom order whetstones from Arkansas.

How to APPRECIATE KNIVES

The author outlays a novel approach to understanding quality and performance.

By Michael Janich

The knife is a truly extraordinary item. When prehistoric man first learned to use the edge of a sharp stone as a cutting tool more than 2.5 million years ago, our evolution as a species took a giant leap forward. Arguably one of the most important developments in history, the knife subsequently evolved into much more than a tool.

Its roles as a weapon, work of art, status symbol, a feat of engineering, and cultural icon became just as significant. For those new to the world of knives, this simple historical perspective is a great place to start your appreciation of the knife.

To neophytes, the world of knives can be overwhelming. Look through the pages of this book, and you will quickly see the incredibly broad spectrum of cutting tools available today. You will also begin to get a sense of the many niches in the knife world and the passionate, often outspoken personalities that inhabit them.

Approached correctly, that kind of diversity can easily make knives and the culture that surrounds them a lifelong fascination. Taking the first step, however, can be a little intimidating. The secret, like most things in life, is learning how to appreciate.

No matter where you are in your journey through the world of knives, the broader your perspective, the deeper your appreciation of the knife will become. To help guide you in that process, let us look at the different approaches you can take to deepen your appreciation of knives.

The Utilitarian Approach

One of the best ways to appreciate knives is to use them. If you have never carried a knife before, invest in one that comfortably fits your budget and commit to carrying it every day. When an appropriate task presents itself, use your knife to solve the problem.

Whether it is cutting a stray thread, opening a package, or sharpening a pencil, using your knife regularly as possible will help establish its value as a tool in your mind. Soon you will wonder how you ever got along without one.

Depending on the type of knife you choose initially and the chores you tackle with it, you will probably begin to realize that different tasks are best performed with certain kinds of knives. If your starter model is a Swiss Army Knife with large and small blades, you will discover that detailed tasks like picking splinters are easier using a small blade, while cutting a piece of rope is a job for a bigger knife.

Furthering that concept, look for opportunities to use purpose-designed knives in context. Filet a fish with a well-designed filet knife, and you will quickly appreciate why it has a narrow, flexible blade. Use a hawkbill utility blade to cut a few pieces of carpet-

ing, and you will understand why it is shaped the way it is.

If you are the type who has always used a serrated steak knife to dice vegetables, try it with an actual chef's knife (and some proper instruction) and discover the difference the right knife can make. Understanding why knives are shaped differently to perform specific tasks is an excellent way of learning to appreciate them as tools.

Performance Matters

We have all heard the saying, "You get what you pay for," and most of us have plenty of life experiences to validate it. When it comes to knives, this concept is often the bridge between inexpensive, entry-level knives and understanding—and appreciating— what real quality and performance are all about.

Whatever knife you carry and use now, compare it to the one you had before. If your current model is your first, set a goal to make your next knife an upgrade. The idea is to have a basis of comparison

Above: One of the easiest ways to start appreciating knives is to carry one and use it every chance you get. This Spyderco Delica 4 Wharncliffe is one of the author's daily carry knives.

Right: Good knives offer performance that lesser-quality ones do not. The only way to appreciate that is to try a blade better than you have now. This Murray Carter-designed Bunka Spyderco Bocho model performs well beyond a typical chef's knife.

Various cultures of the world often have specific knives associated with them. Exploring the diversity of these cutting tools is a great way to appreciate the tools themselves.

between a good knife and a better model that allows you to quantify the difference.

Whether it takes a better edge, holds it longer, cuts cleaner, opens smoother, feels better in your hand, or carries more comfortably, take the time to understand its attributes. Then, translate that quality level into the difference in cost between the two. This process will help you appreciate the value of individual knives and the larger scale quality differences between brands, designers, and makers.

The Gadget Factor

Knives, specifically folding knives, are a fantastic canvas for mechanical innovation. Just as all watches ultimately tell time, folders, once open, all cut and puncture things. How they open, however, is where the magic happens.

You can appreciate the mechanical aspects of folding knives on a basic level through their evolution from simple friction folders to slip joints and lock blades. You can then dive deep into the various types of locking mechanisms, their advantages, disadvantages, and effects on the knives' design parameters.

From an engineering standpoint, you can crawl inside the details of the mechanisms and strive to understand exactly how they work and function, comparing each of their components. In the

Many knives also have a strong "gadget factor." The balisong is a prime example of this, whether, from left to right, a traditional version made in the Philippines, a Darrel Ralph custom Venturi or an antique French penknife.

Some knives are technological marvels. The limited-edition Hogue double-action out-the-front automatic (top) is a mechanical masterpiece. For its time, the old-school Bonsa trapdoor single-action out-the-front auto offered the same mystique.

process, you can consider the tolerances of the parts, how they affect each lock's intended function, and the level of craftsmanship necessary to make a mechanism work properly.

As your understanding of different mechanisms deepens, you may find favorites that inspire themes for your interest and collection. For example, the Filipino balisong has a brilliantly simple locking mechanism that allowed native craftsmen who used hand tools to make it. Its twin-handled design also allows the operator to open, close, and manipulate it in countless ways. To me, that makes every expression of the balisong worthy of appreciation, from the crudest handmade versions to expensive production and custom models.

To truly embrace the concept of knives as mechanical marvels, consider looking at automatics and the incredible ingenuity of their designs. Although they all do the same thing—the blades spring open at the push of buttons—how they accomplish that is an astonishingly deep rabbit hole of knife design and history. Some breeds of switchblades, like double-action out-the-front autos, are nothing short of magical in the precision of their operation.

Knives as Cultural Icons

The knife's critical role in the evolution of humankind has made it an integral part of many cultures. The world is filled with thousands of distinctive ethnic knife designs inspired by the people, cultures, religions, and traditions that created them.

Exploring this family of knives is an outstanding way of enhancing your appreciation of edged tools, as you will learn about much more than the knives themselves; you will understand the heart, souls, and values of the people who created them.

From a collector's perspective, purchasing genuine ethnic knives can sometimes be challenging and expensive. However,

many companies specialize in crafting authentic reproductions that are reasonably priced.

Some manufacturers and custom makers also express iconic cultural designs in modern form, paying homage to their origins while pushing the envelope of knives as an art form.

Even if you choose not to collect cultural knives, understanding the deep significance they had—and still have—to many societies will quickly deepen your appreciation of cutting tools in general.

Knives as Weapons

Aside from clubs and other striking weapons, knives, and by extension, swords, axes, and similar cutting tools are among the oldest weapons known to man. When someone trusts his life to something, he tends to have strong opinions about its form and function. Throughout history, this has led to the development of an astonishing array of edged weapons, each with its own

Knives explicitly designed for military use, like this classic Randall Model 18, have special significance in the world of cutlery.

The best way to appreciate knives is to understand the people who create them. In the first image, the "Godfather of Tactical Knives," Bob Terzuola (third from left in beige "History" shirt and standing behind the counter) chats with the man who defined the form of the modern folding knife, Spyderco founder Sal Glesser (directly facing Turzuola at right). Glesser (left) engages accomplished custom knifemaker Jot Singh Khalsa (right) in a conversation in the second photo.

compelling story.

From a military perspective, knives and swords have not only been weapons of warfare, but they have also become powerful symbols of rank and unit identity. Like the Fairbairn-Sykes commando dagger, the First Special Service Force's V-42, and the Gurkha Kukri, many iconic designs have achieved legendary status far beyond their actual use in combat.

Like Bo Randall of Randall Knives and John Ek, several legendary knifemakers were also instrumental in developing knife designs specifically for close combat. The stories behind these designs, their manufacture, and the men who carried them into battle are an amazing niche of military history and a sure way to bolster your love of knives.

Similarly, knives and other edged weapons have been closely associated with various martial arts and self-defense systems for centuries. The tactics of those systems often reflected, and sometimes relied upon, specific design characteristics of the knives.

One famous example of this breed is the karambit, which traces its history back to a Southeast Asian agricultural tool. Still, it is best known as a signature weapon of martial arts like Indonesian pencak silat.

The pommel ring found on many styles of karambit allows it to be spun on the user's index finger to extend its range and allow pulling cuts. Whether in its traditional form or more modern fixed-blade and folding adaptations, understanding its history and evolution is the doorway to appreciating a unique design.

Knives sometimes transcend the role of tools to become true works of art. Renowned custom knifemaker Allen Elishewitz is also a master of the art of guilloché—a unique style of machine engraving—as evidenced by this exquisite version of his "Tactician" folder.

Knife Tech

In today's world, people are more tech-savvy than ever before. For those who enjoy getting lost in the minutiae, knives offer a deep rabbit hole. In addition to the mechanical aspects of their construction mentioned earlier, today's production knives come in a spectacular array of materials.

On a basic level, you can focus on handle materials and delve into the functional and aesthetic differences between laminates like G10, Micarta®, and carbon fiber and state-of-the-art metals like titanium.

If you are incredibly ambitious, however, you can explore the nuances of blade steels. Start with traditional carbon steels and conventional ingot stainless steels to understand the basics of metallurgy and heat treating. Once you have wrapped your head around that, dig into the dynamics of powder metallurgy, exotic alloy mixes, carbide volumes, and all the other details that define modern high-tech steels.

Many fans of hi-tech toys cannot resist customizing, modifying, and accessorizing their prized possessions. If that sounds like you, once again, you are in luck. Whether you want to add a simple fob and pewter bead to your knife or trick it out with custom scales and a color-anodized deep-pocket titanium clip, there is a vendor out there who makes what you want.

Knives as Art

One obvious way of appreciating knives is to look at them as pieces of art. At a basic level, factory knives are impressive examples of industrial design, and, just like cars and watches, many brands have a signature look all their own.

Handmade knives range from spartan, utilitarian designs to highly sophisticated pieces that are just as much sculpture as cutting tools. In addition to their meticulous craftsmanship, custom knives can also feature all manner of functional and artistic embellishments. They might be hand-forged, clay tempered, or even crafted with layered damascus steel.

Further, you can manipulate the damascus to create a spectacular array of patterns or even intricate mosaic designs.

Makers craft handles of almost every material imaginable, with popular choices including exotic hardwoods, horn, and mother of pearl. Any metal component of the knife is also a potential surface for embellishment, including decorative file work, engraving, and even inlaying with precious metals.

Equally stunning sheaths usually complement art-quality fixed blades, often crafted from premium leather, exotic animal skins, and other rare materials.

The People

The ultimate way to appreciate knives is to get to know the people who create them, sell them, and collect them. Researching the history of legendary figures like Bo Randall, Robert W. Loveless, Bill Moran, Col. Rex Applegate, Blackie Collins, Al Mar, A.G. Russell, and the other pioneers of the industry is a great start.

Understanding the profound influence of living legends like Sal Glesser, Ernest Emerson, Ken Onion, and Chris Reeve will deepen that perspective and provide a sense of how profound one person's influence on the form and function of modern knives can be.

Building on that foundation, talk to custom knifemakers and ask them about their artistic approach to crafting knives. Similarly, engage knife designers, collectors, and dealers in conversation, and learn what motivates and inspires them.

Join Internet forums and social media groups devoted to knives and share in the passion of their members. You will soon realize that every design, blade shape, lock mechanism, damascus pattern, and literally every knife-related idea started with someone worth knowing and appreciating.

That human element has been the driving force in the evolution of knives for their entire history. Be grateful for that, and your appreciation of knives will know no bounds. □

Some of the people who have shaped the knife community are true legends, like the late Col. Rex Applegate, close-combat instructor for the Office of Strategic Services (OSS, the predecessor of the CIA) in World War II. Shown at top-left is the prototype of his iconic Applegate-Fairbairn Folder, and at right is an autographed first-production model from Gerber.

Whiskey & Me:
Story of a Special Dog Immortalized

Master smith forges blades from canine's chain and cremated ashes at the owner's request.

By Steve Schwarzer, American Bladesmith Society master smith
All images by Andreas Kalani

Andreas Kalani and his K9 training partner, Whiskey Boy, take a break in the knife shop. After 11 years of Red Cross search-and-rescue and protection training and forming a forever bond, Andreas lost his dog family member. Andreas asked American Bladesmith Society master smith Steve Schwarzer to help him forge Whiskey's dog chain and cremated ashes into knife blades.

*J*n the flow of life, we get to meet only a few people and animals that positively change our direction. These profound connections are generally not expected but rather happen as a matter of course.

I have had this experience in my life several times, both as a youth and adult. The emotional response to such chance meetings changed me at a core level. These beings appeared in my life seemingly at just the right moments.

The profound experiences were not always with humans. I have always had an emotional attachment to pets. I owned crows, raccoons, possums, snakes, turtles, squirrels, armadillos, cats, and many dogs over 73 years of life. Like my buddy, Bob, says, unless you call its name and it comes to you, it is not a pet. That always made me laugh. So, dogs it is.

I have had the pleasure of sharing life with many canine friends. Nothing responds to kindness like a dog, and nothing forgives quicker. One remarkable dog was a blue healer named Squeak. A 17-year buddy, and shop dog I raised from a puppy, brought a lot of joy into my life. Squeak was the ultimate shop dog and always a great source of amusement. If you threw a ball, he would lie there with a look that said, "Nice throw."

I trained him to sit on a stump and jump into my arms on command. It was hilarious until one night, I walked from my shop to the house in the dark with a tray full of hot food, and Squeak decided he would perform that trick without prompting. You can imagine the result.

This type of memory about the excited response of a loving dog makes us struggle hard not to add anamorphic characteristics to the bond. Man and dog have worked as a team for over 100,000 years. Dogs were depicted in rock art hunting with humans thousands of years ago, and they are part of our family, and we should treat them as such.

Many in the knife community got to meet Squeak during his long tenure in my shop and life. When he passed, it was extremely painful, and it took many years before I could allow myself another dog.

The story I share with you is a personal journey of another incredible dog and a special man. It starts with a phone call from a gentleman I briefly visited at the last BLADE Show West in Portland, Oregon. He was referred to me by a mutual friend who figured I was a good fit for an unusual project he had in mind.

Top: Before we could forge it into canister steel, we first cleaned the chain collar using an acetylene torch. We sandblasted it, then heated it to remove all the chrome plating.
Right: After burning the chrome off the steel chain, we dipped it into an acid bath as just one more step in the process to assure success. The goal was to forge a knife blade that would incorporate and show the pattern of the original dog collar.
Left: When Whiskey came into Andreas Kalani's life, he was a 20-pound ball of fur.

Brilliant Artist

Andreas Kalani is a brilliant artist and knifemaker. He immigrated many years ago from Persia as a young man and started developing his unique artwork and knives. Like Andreas's artwork, his character is also exceptional. He is a team player, a characteristic I greatly admire in humans. Andreas has an unstoppable creative side and an enormous drive that pushes him to develop art in several mediums.

The mediums cover skills as diverse as designing websites, creating graphic art, experimenting with other electronic pallets, and a great understanding of casting resins and metals. His forging skills are fantastic, and Andreas' unique style blends metal skills with what he refers to as "natural universe," a technique that you must see to believe (view his knife in the "Handle Craft" chapter within the "State of the Art" section of this book). The resulting knives are dioramas of nature and the universe.

Andreas emigrated from a currently harsh area that dates to the dawn of history. He has expressed his extreme gratitude to me and others for his opportunity and place in this country. His willingness to give back to the community ultimately led him to train as a Red Cross first responder, where he found the wildfire and search-and-rescue K9 programs of great interest. Working with the dogs in rescue and protection was right up his alley.

In 2008, Andreas sought a K9 training partner and was looking for a standard German Shepherd breed when a friend sent him an ad, as a joke, touting "hybrid wolf puppies." He was intrigued by the wolf concept and contacted the lady placing the ad, who sent a picture of a black-and-white furball. The dog was 75 percent Mackenzie Valley wolf (Northwestern wolf), 12.5 percent Swedish shepherd, and 12.5-percent Alaskan Malamute.

Ten weeks later, the 20-pound furball arrived.

These hybrid wolves are not the dog for an average owner. They require a tremendous amount of socialization activity and training and a 24/7 commitment. In this case, "Whiskey Boy's" arrival was the start of an 11-year bond of inseparable friends. They camped, swam, and trained together constantly, creating a deep bond to which many of us can relate.

When one's life is so intertwined with another being, either human or animal, that it brings such joy of sharing, it is excruciating when one of the players leaves. When I lost my dog of 17 years, it was another 12 before I could allow myself to attach to the next dog partner. I understand the depth of loss.

When I received the phone call from Andreas, we talked at length about his dog, Whiskey Boy, and how painful it was losing such an integral part of his life. After much discussion, we hit upon a plan

---

Top and left: Steve Schwarzer grinds and cleans the canister parts, removing all scale to ensure a good weld. In a later step, he grinds off the sacrificial metal from the canister. Lower right: Steve welds the canister shut in preparation for forging.

to forge a memorial knife that included Whisky Boy, literally. Andreas wanted to make a powder metal canister that would incorporate Whiskey's steel collar, which would still be recognizable as a dog chain when forged into a blade billet.

This task seemed simple on its face, but the forging of a pattern that closely resembles a material's raw form is difficult to accomplish. It is a one-shot deal. You make a mistake, and, in this case, you lose the chain form forever. Andreas did not trust the job to anyone else. No pressure on me!

History of Forging Damascus

I have a long history in the knife industry, primarily in forging damascus, and have always enjoyed a good challenge. Way back, I was one of the first to employ the complex canister technique in which a bladesmith must understand a great deal about the chosen materials to pull it off. The initial research was by trial and error, and that was not an option on this project.

I teach this bladesmith method and have personally forged several hundred knives with canister steel blades.

The project would require a canister, powdered steel, and a bunch of planning and prep to complete, as well as all the skills I could muster. There would be no way to replace the materials incorporated into the powder-damascus canister.

Though greatly honored to be asked to participate in the one-of-a-kind project, it was a little daunting with no room for error. I had to plan every step, leaving no detail to chance. Andreas thought it was so important to him. He got on a plane and flew to Florida from California with the chain in hand.

My wife, Lora, and I met Andreas at the airport in Daytona Beach. The hour drive to my shop and home gave us some valuable planning time to get the project underway. These were the first few building blocks of a long friendship.

We started with components and expectations. When Andreas had his Whiskey Boy cremated, he

Top: Schwarzer forge welds the assembled canister.
Middle: Whiskey works hard on his protection training.
Lower: Andreas Kalani (left) and Steve Schwarzer take a shop selfie.

had saved the remains. I asked Andreas to bring some of the ashes. I had, in my past, seen several times where people had incorporated ash remains into memorials. Several prominent blacksmiths and bladesmiths have had their ashes run through a forge. Andreas and I decided on a plan to include the ashes and Whiskey Boy's chain into two canisters.

The first canister was to include the chain. Unfortunately, it was not a matter of wadding up the chain, putting it in a box, and adding powdered steel like in some typical down-and-dirty projects. Still, the initial canister required a bunch of preparation on the chain before we could use it. It was steel, factory-chrome-plated chain, and I needed to remove all that plating. That alone was no easy task. I burned the chrome coating, then submerged the chain in acid to remove every trace of contamination that could prevent it from self-forging in the canister. I also sandblasted the chain after neutralizing it in the acid bath.

The next step required us to carefully fold the chain to appear as chain links in the blade billet after billet forging. We decided the chain might move out of place before welding the powdered steel, so we cut it in sections and tack-welded them together.

Lighting the Forge

We built a custom canister out of a mild steel sheet in which to fit the chain. After carefully folding the chain and packing the powdered steel in and around it, we sealed up the canister with a weld, added a handle, and prepared to light the forge.

Once we had the forge up to temperature, we placed the canister in the fire. The welding process went flawlessly, but the real test would be when we opened the package. The pattern-welded steel billet turned out great. Although not perfect, we could see the forge-welded chain links. Additional distortion caused by the blade forging further distorted the pattern a bit.

The second canister contained high-carbon steel powder and Whiskey Boy's ashes. That canister was also well planned, though not nearly as complicated as forging the chain, and it also went without a hitch. Still, it was a make-or-break project.

We videotaped much of the process and managed to get two knife blades out of the resulting steel.

Top: Schwarzer saws off the end of the canister to check for success during the forge-welding operation.
Lower images: Whiskey cools off near a creek. Sitting solo, this highly trained dog didn't move unless commanded.

The finished blades incorporate Whiskey's cremated ashes and chain collar.

The one with the chain still shows the pattern. The other is pure Whiskey. Andreas was assembling the knives as I was writing this article.

He spent a week in Florida with Lora and me, and we shared fantastic time healing wounds and forging new friendships. After sharing several hard days at the forge and many evenings in the kitchen and cooking meals on the grill, we built a pile of memories that will last a lifetime. We shared stories and tears about our lost pets, and I was about 10 pounds heavier after Andreas left than when he arrived in Florida. He is an amazing cook, and we grilled a different style of kabob almost every evening.

Andreas flew back to California with a lot of painful weight off his shoulders. He and I have since added new dogs to our lives. There is nothing like having that hollow spot in your heart filled.

The knives are a permanent memorial to Whiskey and a constant reminder of time spent with a truly unique dog. Andreas and I shared many stories and laughter about the great times we had with our dog family members. If you have ever loved an animal, you can relate. The pictures herein tell the story. □

Top right: Steve uses dies in the Chambersburg power hammer to consolidate the canister.
Middle left: Heat cleaning the chain was a crucial part of the preparation.
Middle right and lower: As they were always together in life, Andreas Kalani ensured he and his dog, Whiskey, would be together after the canine's death by having its steel dog collar and cremated ashes forged into knife blades.

STRANGE AND UNUSUAL

They are not the weirdest knives ever made, but they point toward the eclectic.

Text and images by David W. Jung

Who decides what is peculiar, unusual, or even strange and weird in a knife? Ultimately it is you. When a company comes out with a knife, they have a market in mind. Who is the end-user? Are we making this knife for the gizmo collector who will never use it? Will it be a knife that is unusual yet still appeals to the everyday user market?

Answers to these questions will determine the success of the knife. Will it be a "weird" little knife that hardly gets any attention or a bestseller?

Throughout history, humans have displayed ingenuity through the creation of edged tools. For each handcrafted knife, there was often someone who wanted to take the design to a new level. Sometimes it would be a modification that improved function for the task at hand. Other times, the change would reflect a creative desire to explore the boundary of art versus practicality.

The original Spyderco Worker was a revolutionary knife when Sal Glesser introduced it in 1981. The knife incorporated a pocket clip and an odd blade shape with a hole that allowed for one-hand opening. While one-hand opening is commonplace today, at the time, it was a novel idea in folders.

Designed by Joe Flowers, the Condor Otzi is inspired by a small flint knife discovered next to Otzi, "The Iceman," who died 3,000 years ago. Explorers discovered his frozen remains in the mountains bordered by Austria and Italy.

When a creation improved the knife DNA, others would copy it. When the new design reflected an artistic choice outside of the norm, no one would widely reproduce it without profit potential. Since the earliest days, the cost of production compared to return has shaped artistic design.

The earliest knives were chipped rock, sharpened bone, or repurposed natural items like sharp animal claws or fangs. Early man saw the advantage of sharp by observing animal behavior. This learning process influenced tool creation, which was vital in establishing mastery over a harsh environment. Early knives acted as force multipliers in fighting for survival, hunting, and building primitive tools and shelter.

The use of tools by our ancestors allowed for efficiency, which in turn led to creativity. Early craftsmen began to create edged tools that were as beautiful as they were functional. As society grew, the highest quality tools would often go to the tribal leaders as tribute or show status.

Fast forward to today, and rare or unusual knives are no longer reserved for the wealthy. While there are one-off jewelry knives that cost thousands of dollars, they are unlikely to cut anything. Fortunately, due to the widespread use of CNC (computer numerically controlled) mass production, the ordinary knife user can afford many unique knives that push the boundary of what might be called an everyday user.

Flavor Over Function?

It is essential to define what makes one knife a basic everyday user and another an oddity. A sharp blade with a handle is the start, but details of the

One-piece knives with integral, ergonomic handles are uncommon because of high production costs. The rustproof David Boye Basic Knife (left) is cast from dendritic cobalt metal using the lost-wax process, while the Cold Steel Drop Forged Hunter (center) is 52100 steel with a 4-inch blade. At right, the Chris Reeve Knives "Aviator" is machined from a solid billet of A2 tool steel.

design can improve function or add enough flavor to make the knife unique.

For this discussion, we will limit the scope of knives to those that are in factory production, or if discontinued, available in the secondary market. It is too easy to find strange one-off custom knives that are unusual but not reproducible or available in production quantity.

Two companies have an outsize presence when discussing unique knives. Columbia River Knife & Tool (CRKT) of Portland, Oregon, and Spyderco of Golden, Colorado, have produced many knives that one would call unusual. From the original Spyderco Worker model, which was very much outside of the box, to the CRKT Provoke, both companies have pushed the boundaries of what might be considered a normal knife.

When asked why Spyderco is willing to take on unique knife designs, Marketing and Communications Manager Joyce Laituri said, "Innovation happens in unusual places. There are very few 'firsts' in the knife industry. When Spyderco encounters innovation, imagination, and a willingness to try something new, we often take up the challenge.

"The owners of Spyderco, Sal and Gail Glesser, have always taken the road less traveled, and that is a compliment," Laituri assures.

CRKT has brought several unique knives to the market and excelled with many great production pieces that would be unobtainable or above the average knife user's budget in their original hand-made custom versions. Being able to afford distinct

Above: A gizmo knife has a high fidget factor or an amusing operating mechanism. Some knives have both attributes. Designed by Ed Halligan, the Columbia River Knife & Tool (CRKT) K.I.S.S. (bottom and middle-right models), which stands for Keep It Super Simple, has been a popular two-piece knife with a unique one-side blade grind. The CRKT Snap-Lock (top and middle-left) by Ed Van Hoy sports an equally unique swing-out blade. The knives are offered in models of varying sizes and blade and handle finishes.

knives enriches our collecting universe.

Blade shape and construction are the most visible attributes that one notices when looking at a knife. Even the earliest steel blade designs would not look out of place today. Many blade patterns have been around for hundreds of years, demonstrating the excellence of the original designs.

Left: The TOPS Knives Tom Brown Tracker survival knife is available in several sizes and blade finishes. What makes the knife unusual is the curved chopping fore blade with a recessed secondary edge. Brown's Tracker was featured in the 2003 film, "The Hunted."

Culture of Cut

Ethnic blade shapes, such as the Japanese tanto, Filipino kris, and the Nepalese kukri, are recognizable on many modern production knives. Each culturally significant design has been adapted to domestic standards, which often include a reduction in size along with the use of modern knife steel.

Thus, you can also see the traditional tanto tip found on samurai swords mirrored on many modern production blades. Is a knife unusual when a maker produces 500,000 copies? At some point, it becomes just another knife pattern.

The thin, upswept blade of the CRKT Ritual, designed by Alan Folts, reminds one of a classic Persian knife pattern remade using modern materials like Sandvik 12C27 steel and a white fiber-resin handle. Is it practical? Hard to say. Is it unique? Yes.

The Cold Steel Kiridashi is a solid attempt to reinterpret a classic ethnic knife—the Japanese Kiridashi craft—into a modern folding knife.

Another area that can make a knife stand out is the choice of blade material. When knifemakers introduced the first ceramic blade knives, they were revolutionary. Even though there were limitations due to the lack of blade flexibility, they represented a novel approach to blade chemistry. The reintroduction of damascus, credited mainly to knifemaker Bill Moran in the 1970s, further increased the blade palate available to knife companies, with pattern-welded steel featured in limited production knives today.

Knifemaker David Boye brought another unique cutting material to the industry: dendritic cobalt blades that are cast rather than forged or ground. The suspended carbides within the cobalt provide a toothy cutting edge while providing a rust-free blade.

If we are living in a golden age of knifemaking, some credit must go to the makers of high-performance particle-metal steels and nitrogen-based metals. Exotic steels have allowed knife users access to technologically advanced stainless blades, though the price tag is slightly higher than traditional high-carbon steel.

Material Mashup

Will blade material choice make a knife rare? It can if it is a unique variation that is limited in quantity. And often, a unique combination of blade materials or features that might not be in vogue can later

The Spyderco Dodo is the first production knife Eric Glesser designed. Each original version incorporated a CPM S30V blade and a Ball Bearing Lock™, a metal ball in a track that secured the folder open. Despite the odd appearance, the Dodo Knife is comfortable and functional.

Credit card knives range from one-piece blades like the Microtech (top row, second from right) and Simbatec (far right, middle row) models to folding blade designs like the Spyderco Spydercard (second from right in bottom row), the Zootility Tools WildCard (bottom-left) and Sinclair Cardsharp (second from left in the top and third rows). The thin plastic case of the Victorinox SwissCard (top-left and second row, second from left) houses a blade and tools reminiscent of the Victorinox Classic. Wallet knives are great backup tools for emergencies.

soar to new heights in the collectible market. How a folder opens or closes and its blade locking mechanism can provide fertile ground for innovation. Grant and Gavin Hawk, designers of the Kershaw E.T. with its External Toggle lock (thus the name "E.T."), are great examples of knifemakers who think outside the box. Companies like Benchmade, Cold Steel, CRKT, Kershaw, Spyderco, and others have produced many attractive folding knife lock designs.

The unusually shaped Spyderco Dodo with its Ball Lock™ and the CRKT Provoke that employs a Kinematic® system are excellent examples of unique opening and locking mechanisms.

Above all, an opening system or lock must be functional enough for everyday use. One person's easy-to-use lock might be impossible for someone with larger or smaller hands to manipulate and use.

Handle form allows for even more design creativity than blade shape. While ergonomics is important, there is a wide range of artistic handle designs that work equally well. Some handles appear entirely uncomfortable, but when put into practical use, they feel great. This design irony can result in exciting handle forms and shapes.

The limited-production WE Knife Company Eschaton model, designed by Elijah Isham, is an example of an extreme futuristic blade and handle design that is surprisingly comfortable to grip and use. Of carbon fiber and titanium construction, the Eschaton is lightweight for its size. The reasonably priced folder quickly sold out, and secondary-market values are climbing. Fortunately, the similar WE Knife Company Arrakis model is still available in a similar price range.

Knives do not have to be black and silver. Through technological advances, new handle scale materials can also lead to wild colors and unique tactile hand purchase. Companies like Case Knives have been using brilliantly colored Kirinite™ acrylic handles on many of their traditional patterns. Adept at marketing to knife collectors, Case has successfully embraced many handle materials to feed collector desires. Companies like Benchmade and Spyderco are just two of many manufacturers that have created multiple handle color variations for their knife buyers.

Far Out Fixed Blades

Creative design is not limited to folders. The Tom Brown Tracker series from TOPS Knives shows how a fixed blade can perform many functions in

Above: Designed by Alan Folts, the CRKT Ritual melds a traditional blade shape with modern technology. It sports a 4.37-inch, Persian-style Sandvik 12C27 blade, but unlike its ancient predecessors, the Ritual blade works off an assisted-opening mechanism and a LinerLock.

Left: The traditional Japanese model of the same name inspired the Cold Steel Kiridashi, a craft knife commonly used for scribing and woodworking. The Cold Steel version strays from the original with a 4034SS blade ground on both sides and a sturdy Tri-Ad® lock designed by Andrew Demko.

the confines of a knife format. The Tracker boasts survival knife qualities such as ax-like chopping performance.

Other far-out fixed blades are machined or stamped one-piece integrals. Those with integrally constructed blades and handles include the Chris Reeve One Piece knives, Cold Steel Drop Forged Series, David Boye Cobalt Basic Knives, and the Ka-Bar Forged Wrench knife. Though they have fewer parts, integral knives can get pricy due to production setup and machining costs.

Knives like the CRKT K.I.S.S., designed by Ed Halligan, are examples of folders that attracted gizmo knife buyers who prefer to use blades for their intended purposes. With its unique tanto blade ground on one side only and an opposite-sided supporting frame, the K.I.S.S. has been an enormous success. Though there are many K.I.S.S. knives in enthusiasts' hands, there are also variations that would fall into the rare category. These include a Japanese-made Shiny K.I.S.S. with satin finish and polished silver and black versions featuring gold trim. This design is an example of how limited-run variations of a popular knife can achieve advanced collector status.

The Ed Van Hoy Snap Lock, made by CRKT, is another gizmo knife that looks like something out of a Jules Verne novel. It certainly takes on the steampunk aesthetic in a well-machined package. Pressure on a knob actuates a cam that spreads the handle halves apart to unlock the blade, which rotates in and out of a V-shaped frame. As with the K.I.S.S., the Snap

If you had to pick the most futuristic production knife available, the WE Knife Company Eschaton, designed by Elijah Isham, would have to be one of the top contenders. The limited-production Eschaton flipper quickly sold out thanks to its carbon fiber and titanium construction with an M390 blade. Fortunately, a similar Arrakis model, also designed by Isham, is available for enthusiasts.

lock comes in several limited-run editions. If there is a genuine steampunk knife aesthetic, the Snap Lock is at the top of the list.

Figural knives take on animal or human forms. Early examples date back to the ancient Egyptian, Persian, Roman, and Viking periods. Not adding to knife functionality, the artistic renderings symbolized an owner with wealth and power. Since the earliest knives were purpose-designed for hunting or battle, figural knives often took the forms of lions and other powerful beasts.

The Spyderco Pochi, designed by Japanese custom knifemaker Kazuyuki Sakurai, represents a figural knife. In this case, the creature inspiring its design is not a ferocious animal but rather a cute puppy. Unlike many bargain-price figural knives that incorporated inexpensive blade steel and stamped handles, the Pochi has a premium 1.58-inch CPM S45VN blade with a titanium frame lock. Though diminutive in size, it is a capable cutter. With the folding blade fully open, the Pochi resembles a small dog, and whether by design or chance, it looks like a small whale when closed.

Japanese custom knifemaker Kazuyuki Sakurai designed the Spyderco Pochi™ model, shaped like a small dog with the blade open and based on the maker's custom knife series. With a 1.58-inch blade machined from CPM S45VN, the Pochi is a small knife with a movable "tail" that provides a solid grip. As a figural knife, it is unique for being constructed of high-end materials, unlike most figural pieces that tend to be inexpensive novelty items.

Left: The polymer Sekki Paper Knife (lower right), designed by Japanese designer Hiroki Yasuda, is shown here surrounded by representations of yesterday's cutting tools. Yasuda designed it for light-duty paper cutting, and the innovation is in taking the flaked design of primitive knives and reinterpreting it with a high-tech faceted design. At 4.6 inches and 1.2 ounces, you grip the Sekki minus any handle.

Inset: Designed by Joe Caswell, the CRKT Provoke™ takes a traditional Karambit design and incorporates a unique Kinematic™ opening system that resembles a parallelogram with swinging vertices. Designed to be held with the ring up, pressing on the lever via the thumb allows the knife to pivot open quickly. With a 2.41-inch D2 blade, the 6.1-ounce Provoke is a robust cutter.

Confiscated Credit Card Knives

When you examine bins of confiscated airport knives, it becomes evident that "credit card" knives are over-represented. Perhaps it is easy to forget to remove concealed knives in the wallet before boarding an airplane. Designed to slide into a wallet and to take up the same amount of space as a credit card, they represent some of the cleverest knives ever made.

A few credit card knives, like the discontinued Spyderco Spydercard, designed by the late Eduard Bradichan-sky, resemble a pocketknife flattened in a hydraulic press when the blade is open and a credit card with the edge nestled in the frame. Others, such as the widely copied and counterfeited Cardsharp 2 knife, designed by Iain Sinclair of 1980s Timex-Sinclair Computer fame, represent a novel origami-style folding structure.

The Victorinox Swisscard approaches the concept of a wallet knife through a credit card-sized case designed to hold all the tools found in a Swiss Army Classic knife.

Taking the ultra-light approach is the Zootility Wildcard knife. The Wildcard has a thin metal frame and a small blade that swivels on a central pivot. Like the CRKT K.I.S.S., the blade is ground on one side only, with the flat side lying on the frame in the closed position. Along with other credit card designs, the knives achieve their desired function in varied creative approaches.

What makes a knife unique comes down to form and function. A blade that operates unexpectedly, takes on an unusual shape, or is fashioned from non-standard materials could be considered an oddity. Knives like the Japanese-made Sekki Paper Knife, designed by Hiroki Yasuda, re-imagines a primitive flint-knapped hand tool into a futuristic faceted polymer shape. Sekki, in Japanese, translates to "stone tool" in English.

Knives like the original Spyderco Worker represented a break from pocketknife normalcy with novel one-handed opening (standard across the knife industry today). Models such as the CRKT K.I.S.S. are not defined solely by their sales numbers. And they do not inspire direct copies because of inadequate patent protection. Instead, they encourage other makers to create new versions of the peculiar designs.

The design architecture is the first aspect of an unusual knife, while function and finish complete the package. It is impossible to have a definitive list of knives defined as unique or unusual. It is up to the observer to make their own decision.

Fortunately, there are many knife designers and makers that excel at exploring their creative sides. While we might be in the golden era for knife design, all that is possible remains, and we are limited only by our imaginations. □

BILLHOOKS
BEAT A PATH
FROM ITALY

Lost in antiquity, found in ubiquity, the knife is largely unfamiliar to Americans!

By Roderick T. Halvorsen

From top to bottom are the Angelo B "Sorrento[...]
"Double-Edge," Rinaldi "Varese," and Falci "Ro[...]
billhooks the author had the pleasure of using a[...]

Many things likely pop into mind when the average American thinks about Italy. Certainly, bold red wine, sunshine, and pasta must be at the forefront of association with the country. Outdoorspeople would undoubtedly add mountain boots

But even the most knife-savvy American [...] probably not associate "The Boot" with a blac[...] culture such as East Asian countries where [...] parangs, or dahs abound. And yet, there it is [...] ent among farmers, foresters, vintners, gard[...] hunters, and hikers from the timbered slope[...]

While overall tapers of the billhooks vary, all models are of stick-tang construction with the ends peened over pommels or, in the case of the Double-Edge (second from left), its wooden grip. Note the C-style pommels or hand stops on the other three models.

Demands of local flora and the specific needs of agriculture have resulted in a wide variety of heavy Italian knives named for their native regions. No one can pinpoint precisely why specific blade shapes developed, and thus it seems safe to say that details have been lost in antiquity, even while you can find the knives themselves in ubiquity!

Indeed, high-density polyethylene Italian billhooks have been around for a long time. Several companies in Italy still produce a wide range of billhook shapes and sizes. Fortunately, the owners of Baronyx Knife Company and Howland Tools—Benjamin Bouchard and Steven Howland, respectively—were most helpful in providing samples of billhooks for testing.

The companies offer a wide range of Italian billhooks. I tested products from Cav. MARIO VALSECCHI & Figli s.r.l. (also known as [a.k.a.] Angelo B), Falci S.r.l. (a.k.a. Falci) and F.LLI Rinaldi di Rinaldi Faustino & C. snc (a.k.a. Rinaldi).

It took the author four minutes to chop through a 9-inch-thick pine tree—not bad for using one-hand brush knives or billhooks.

I turned these billhook models loose on brush, bramble, and bull pine:
- Angelo B "Sorrento"
- Rinaldi "Varese"
- Falci "Roma"
- Falci "Double-Edge"

For centuries, local 'smiths forged the types of Italian billhooks popular in their regions. Then, an amalgamation of makers took place in 1921, resulting in the Falci corporation, with the Angelo B factory dating back to approximately the same period.

Further noteworthy is the ubiquity of the billhook models these companies make. No fewer than 46 models appear on the Angelo B website, and another 39 examples from Rinaldi and Falci add many more yet.

The four Italian billhooks I obtained sport blades forged and left in oxidized states, with a coating of lacquer or varnish on each to protect them from rust.

While tapers vary on the specific models, all are of stick-tang construction with the ends peened over pommels or, in the case of the Double Edge, its wooden grip. Such a method of construction is traditional and of ancient origin.

Common to many agricultural working tools and machetes, edges straight from the factories are rather rough and what might be considered semi-sharpened, the final grinding or honing left to the end-user. For those who prefer their knives shaving sharp out of the box, Bouchard and Baronyx Knife Company offer a honing service. The edges were keen on the two models I received—the Sorrento and Varese. Such a sharpening service would likely prove popular with other end users.

I was glad to see that the Falci Roma and Double-Edge billhooks were ground so that the basic edge angles required no significant amount of material removed. On blades of 9 or more inches in length, it is nice to have the factory do the bulk of the work for you. Falci did.

Falci billhooks are forged from C45 steel, while C60 remains the alloy of choice for Angelo B. There was no steel designation on the Rinaldi models, but I ascertained it was a similar, simple carbon alloy through use and sharpening.

With a Rockwell hardness rating of 43-46RC, the C45 blade of the Falci performed admirably.

The Rinaldi Varese hook performs secondary duty (aside from cutting or chopping) in pulling a tree limb out of the way.

Rough-and-Ready Field Tools

Being rough-and-ready field tools that see hard use and even abuse, such steel proves adequate. The low hardness rating allows for easy sharpening in the field using a file, though the edge held up well on the various cutting media I encountered.

The Angelo B blades rate 57-60RC, yet when employing my test with a worn file, there was not much observable difference between the makes.

As the name of the knife style suggests, each blade is forged with a bill and hook, though in detail, the variation is dramatic. The Varese model possesses the most classic hook, while the Roma and Sorrento bear the least traditional forms, theirs being almost vestigial bumps purpose-designed for cutting tasks long lost to the sands of time. They served many modern purposes, providing a bit of protection as guards against small stones when chopping material on the ground and with enough unsharpened bulk for digging if necessary.

Above: Scabbard styles for billhooks vary from the "bucket" scabbard the author made (top) to the Rinaldi edge guard (center) and Baronyx HDPE (high-density polyethylene) custom sheath (bottom).
Right: A single strike from the Falci Roma was all that was necessary to sever the pine bough.

While the blade shapes may be ancient, the synthetic rubber, wood, and stacked leather handles are not. Stacked leather construction dates to the mid-19th century on Collin's machetes and other U.S. models, though the material is relatively new to Italian knives. According to my research, stacked leather washers were first used for Italian billhook handles after World War II, and in the case of Angelo B, in 1950.

Appropriate wood not being available, the military obtained good quality leather, possibly scraps from the boot industry. My hunch is that soldiers experiencing American military knives with stacked leather handles during the war were the idea's genesis. At any rate, as many who have used knives with leather washer handles would

appreciate, it quickly became the standard and continues its stronghold even after the introduction of synthetic materials.

At the front of the leather grip, in place of a traditional guard or ferrule, is a wide, thick, oversized washer that serves as a handguard. Each of the leather handles on the test knives measures 4.75 inches long and ends in a grip hook or C-style pommel. The design serves its purpose and is appreciated when wearing heavy gloves or mittens or when the arm gets tired, the grip is wet, or the temperatures drop far below freezing, and the hand becomes numb.

Such billhooks are heavy blades and quite dangerous if you misuse them or in an uncontrolled manner. In some cases, positive C-style pommel stops are safety features worthy of note.

Bush and Brush

Wading into the bush and brush, I have carted these heavy knives around now for some time. I used them on my ranch for various chores ranging from trimming a buckthorn tree I should have cut years ago to opening roads clogged by trees fallen during recent windstorms and sweeping light brush from foot trails.

The Angelo B Sorrento is a massive knife. Weighing in at 1 lb., 14.1 oz., with a blade length of 11 inches, it is the heaviest of all those I tested. Blade dimensions were unique in that the thickness was .155 inches at the blade spine nearest the grip and a bit thicker at the tip. The result is quite a hand ax. You grab this cutting tool when you need to chop or split the heaviest material.

I am always skeptical about synthetic grips on heavy knives, but the shape of the Sorrento handle proved comfortable and secure. I rarely found my hand bumping the grip stop, or C-style pommel, at all. The most effective use was on cutting media ¾ inches in diameter or thicker. Due to weight and balance, I found hand and whip speed using the Sorrento a bit lacking for the best efficiency on light materials I encountered.

Moving on to the Varese model, the 12-inch blade has the most pronounced bill and hook of all those tested. At 1 lb., 8.2 oz., the Varese was the second heaviest as well. Sporting a strongly tapered blade, starting with a thickness of .205 inches at the grip and ending at .125 inches nearest the tip, wrist whip was encouraged by the balance, and overall cutting efficiency exceeded expectations. The Varese shined in clearing light, springy, annoying brush that tends to ride up the blade and bounce off the point when struck by convex-ground blades.

As I discovered with two billhooks I forged—and certainly with the hook-nosed Varese—the cutting media tends to build up in the blade's curve, sliding up the edge toward the tip before hitting the inside bend of the blade hook where it is finally caught and cut.

The Varese's hook broke down heavy fir and pine, allowing one to retain a grip on the knife while tossing the boughs aside. The hook made for a handy digger, too, as is common to many edged vegetable harvesting tools. Like the Double-Edge model, one downside to the distinct blade shape is the tendency for the hook to foul or get gummed and jammed up with cutting media when working in tightly packed, thick, woody brush.

With a 9.5-inch blade, the Falci Roma was a

Above: While wood and synthetic billhook handles certainly suffice, the author says there is just something he likes about stacked leather. Left: The perfectly round handle of the Falci Double-Edge was best grasped barehanded or wearing rubber or rubber-faced gloves.

delight to use. Some knives are just plain fun to swing, and this one fits that category. Blade thickness ran .195 inch at the grip and .12 inch at the tip, with the billhook weighing 1 lb., 7.1 oz. This model is the one I would choose as a cutting companion on long hikes where a survival tool may be of use. Cutting properties were quite impressive, satisfactory, though not performing to the level of the Varese on the thin brush. On heavy, thick, dense wood, the cutting ability of the Roma was nearly comparable to the larger models.

Jack of All Trades

The last billhook tested, the Falci Double-Edge, incorporates a 9-inch blade and a 5 7/8-inch handle, weighing in at 1 lb., 6.6 oz. Sporting a blade shape reminiscent of old English models, the Double-Edge was a jack of all trades. While the hooked blade has its advantages, depending on the material, it comes at a price. It can sometimes get in the way of cutting.

As its name implies, the Double-Edge offers a secondary, straight edge on the other side of the blade for just such situations. The simple, round wood handle and a blade thickness of .155 inch at the grip and .135 inch at the tip make this the lightest of the four tested. I thought the round handle might become a tedious thing, allowing the blade to rotate in hand, and in fact, it was more difficult to grasp when wearing thick or leather gloves. When I switched to rubber gloves or used Double-Edge barehanded, I found no disadvantage at all.

The Rinaldi Varese arrived wearing a simple, thin leather edge guard adequate for storage.

Traditional methods of billhook carry include wooden scabbards with shoulder straps or form-fitted sheaths with open backs and thus flaps to secure the blade. Another option is using a "por-taroncola" or "gancio" ("billhook carrier" or "hook"). In this method, a spring steel belt hook allows the user to holster everything from billhooks to machetes and chopping knives. You tote the blades via a simple bent, flat metal hook attached to the belt. Though traditional and common enough, it is not safe, in my opinion, especially for use in places where a person could potentially slip or fall and land on the blade.

I made myself a sort of universal bucket scabbard, allowing easy insertion and extraction of the blade when two hands were needed in tugging and removing brush and boughs.

Benjamin Bouchard at Baronyx Knife Company

Above: Angelo B billhooks adorned with high-visibility green paint await shipment to fill a forestry service contract. *(photo courtesy of Angelo B)*

Right: When the hook of the Double-Edge gets in the way, the flat secondary edge comes in handy.

offers another option, a nicely constructed, form-fitted scabbard made from high-density polyethylene (HDPE) sheeting that appears to be sturdy and light. Such a scabbard would be handy for covering the blade edge when you stuff the billhook in a rucksack (without the unwanted bulk and weight of my bucket sheath).

As an aficionado of heavy knives, I am delighted to have been introduced to the Italian billhooks. I think many others may be as well.

Special thanks to Rosy at Angelo B and Mr. Filippo Prior at Falci for their assistance and information on Italian billhook production and history.

For more information, visit baryonyxknife. com, howlandtools.com, falcitools.com/tools-for-wood/?lang=en, http://www.flli-rinaldi.it/home/, and angelo-b.com. □

MAKE A KNIFE
This Weekend

This crash course helps novices start building knives now!

By Wally Hayes, American Bladesmith Society master smith

In developing this article, I debated whether to explain and demonstrate the forging of a knife or the stock-removal method of blade making. With the novice maker in mind, I chose to build a knife using the stock-removal process. The skill of forging a blade combined with the time constraint inherent in the premise "make a knife this weekend" factored in the decision.

Learning to make a knife using the stock-removal method helps develop skills needed if a novice decides to forge a blade down the road. The feature article also demonstrates to beginners how to achieve temper lines in blades, as I find the practice a lot of fun!

I chose W-2 tool steel for the blade-making process. It is less prone to warping than other steels, clean, and produces excellent temper lines. W-2 steel is available from New Jersey Steel Baron

Shown are tools and supplies needed to "Make a Knife This Weekend." See the complete "List of Tools and Materials Needed" bulleted section herein.

The knife profile is cut out from a steel billet using a fine-tooth hacksaw.

List of Materials and Tools Needed

- W-2 steel billet
- Wenge wood or handle slabs of choice
- Hacksaw
- File
- Scribe
- 4-inch angle grinder
- Hand drill
- 1/8 in. drill bit
- 1/8 in. pinning material (coat hanger, 1/8 in. welding rod or 416 stainless steel rod)
- Imperial high-temperature oven
- Furnace cement
- Sandpaper
- Ferric chloride
- Distilled water
- Ammonia window cleaner
- Peek polishing paste
- Clamps
- Toaster oven
- Magnet
- Roasting pan with a lid and 3 inches of vegetable oil in it
- J-B Weld Kwik five-minute epoxy

If you do not have a forge, I will explain how to turn a barbeque grill into a forge.

Let's Get Started!

I used a marker to draw the shape of the knife on steel, but you can also make cardboard cutouts of different designs and see what appeals to you. Then draw the shape profile of the knife on the steel using the cutouts as a guide.

Cut the blade shape out from the steel billet with a hacksaw. I used a fine-tooth bi-metal blade. These blades work great and cut fast.

Next, put the blade in a vise and file around the edge of the freshly cut profile of the knife. This step removes the hacksaw marks and cleans up the profile, creating straight lines.

Take your marker and blacken the edge entirely around the knife profile. That way, you can scribe a centerline in the exact middle of the steel thickness of the knife and lengthwise completely

(https://newjerseysteelbaron.com).

If novice knifemakers prefer not to make a temper line, O-1 tool steel is a common choice, great steel to work with (I use it a lot), and easy to find at tool supply shops.

I also demonstrate using simple tools to produce an excellent knife instead of having and utilizing a full knifemaking shop.

Safety comes first in making knives. Wear safety glasses and gloves where and when appropriate.

The steel billet size used for this article is 3/16-inch thick by 1 1/4 inches wide and 11 inches long. The shape of the knife is a modern Japanese tanto. You can easily draw up a different blade shape if you like. The blade profile and handle are both tapered to make the overall shape pleasing to the eye.

For the handle, I decided to use two slabs of wenge wood. Each affix to the blade tang with epoxy and three 1/8-inch pins. Wenge wood has soft and hard grains, so when you fashion the handle, you can use a wire brush to produce a cool textured finish. It is fast and easy! I went from 36-grit paper to a wire wheel for a finished look in a couple of minutes. This technique is my nod to my mentor, Don Fogg, who loves wenge wood, but feel free to use what handle material you have available.

The knife profile has been cut out from a steel billet and filed along its edges to smooth the hacksaw marks and straighten all lines.

Use an angle grinder to rough in the blade edges.

around the shape. Use whatever tools you have that will suffice for this step. I used an old set of calipers, but you could use a nail or make a scribe height gauge.

With the calipers, I measured the thickness of the steel, divided by 2, locked the calipers, and scratched a centerline along the thickness of steel around the entire knife profile.

You want the line along what will be the blade edge and the top or spine of the knife. The top line shows the lengthwise center of the blade spine—a ridge that you will shape with a file. This method is typical of Japanese knives and creates an upside-down "V." You can leave this step out if you like. The blade itself will be flat ground and flat filed. Flat grinds are easier for first-time knifemakers.

You have options for creating these flat sides of your blade that taper toward the eventual edge. If you possess a belt sander, great—it makes things go faster—but you do not have to go out and buy one. You could file the flat, tapered sides entirely by hand, which takes a while (I make my apprentices file their first blades).

Grind a Little on One Side, Then …

I used a 4-inch angle grinder for this project. I roughed in the flat sides, tapering them toward the edge evenly on both sides of the blade billet, grinding a little on one side, then a little on the other. This technique prevents overheating the steel on one side, lowering the chance of warpage during the steel heat-treating process.

The angle grinder works great, and I use mine a lot. Make sure to wear protective gear. I have a little bench outside my shop that I clamp my steel onto. You will be finishing the sides flat with a file, so do not scoop out or hollow grind the blade sides.

For the blade flats, I used a Nicholson 10-inch smooth-cut file. Nicholson also offers a file, called the Majicut, with big teeth that shave steel right off the blade. The blade is soft still; any big file will work. I leave the cutting edge about the thickness of a dime before heat treating the steel.

Next up is filing in the top ridge or spine of the blade into a small upside-down "V" shape. Keeping the line of the upper ridge centered lengthwise, file the blade spine down from the ridge, tapering out from the spine and about 1/8-inch down the side of the blade.

Before heat treating the steel, drill three holes in the handle to later secure the wood grips.

Use a marker to draw a centerline on one side of the steel billet horizontally along the length of the handle. Later, you'll drill three holes on that centerline, one in the direct center lengthwise where you will place the wood handle slabs, and the other two holes, also on the centerline, each ¾ inch from each end lengthwise where the wood handles will be secured.

Make a mark for each hole. I center-punch the spots, then drill each 1/8-inch hole with a hand drill or drill press. I counter-sink the holes with a larger diameter drill bit to knock off the corners of the holes.

You will file the bevels into the blade.

Ready for Heat Treating

The knife is now ready to be heat treated.

I planned this project to demonstrate how to heat treat a blade differentially. I used an Imperial high-temperature oven and furnace cement (what I refer to as clay). You can obtain these items at big box hardware stores, or you can omit this step entirely. I find it most rewarding to create a temper line, like making the perfect sourdough crust!

Use a plastic knife to spread the cement along the length of the blade sides. Start at the spine, or ridge of the blade, about a third of the way down each side. In heat treating the steel, the cement, or clay, prevents the top third of the blade from hardening and creates the temper line, or hamon. Differentially heat treating a blade in this way results in a soft, more forgiving blade spine and a hard edge.

You can be as creative as you like, making the bottom cement line, ending a third of the way from the edge, straight or wavy (and thus a straight or wavy temper line or hamon). Also, make sure you cover the spine of the blade with the clay. There are over 200 different temper lines makers have named.

If you are using O-1 tool steel, you will get a straight temper line, as it is a deeper hardening steel (has more alloys in the mix). I use cement on the blade because it makes it easier to straighten the steel billet if it warps during heat treating.

Let the clay dry. Depending on room temperature and if you will be using charcoal or a propane forge on the steel billet, drying time varies. I can apply cement to a blade and put it immediately into my propane forge, but I do not let the clay touch anything in the forge.

If you use a Weber-style charcoal grill, let the clay almost fully harden, so you do not knock it off. A hairdryer speeds up the drying time.

You do not need a high-end propane forge to heat treat a blade. If you have one, great, but I improvised when moving into my new place before building a shop.

Building a Charcoal Forge

To build a charcoal forge, take an old barrel-shaped barbecue grill and cut a

Right: To keep the blade spine soft, harden the edge, and create a temper line. Coat the sides of the steel in fire brick cement, two-thirds of the way down from the spine, before heat treating. The cement prevents the steel underneath from entirely hardening.

The blade is heated up in the forge and ready to quench in vegetable oil.

Drill holes for the handle. For safety purposes, the blade should be clamped down and secured, and it's a good idea to cover the edge when drilling into the wood handle scales.

2-inch-wide slot on each end. Find a piece of 2-inch steel pipe, 4 inches longer than your BBQ. Hammer one end of the pipe closed. Using a ¼-inch bit, drill a straight line of holes along the top of the pipe. The line of holes should stretch about 8 inches long. Insert the pipe through the length of the BBQ, with each end inserted into the 2-inch slots previously cut through to the ends of the old grill.

Find a used blower, hairdryer, or vacuum, and tape the air source to the open end of the pipe, making sure you can easily detach and attach the air source, taking it off and on. You do not want to leave the blower attached and the air off, as the hot, fired-up grill will burn out the blower.

Now, put hardwood charcoal into the BBQ, fire it up, and when it is hot and glowing, attach the blower and turn it on. Grab a scrap piece of tool steel that you hacksawed off your blade. Use some tongs or extra-long plyers to place the steel into the fire.

Grab your magnet, and when the steel is just turning orange, touch the magnet to the steel. If it sticks to the steel, you are not at quenching temperature, and the steel needs to get a bit hotter. When the magnet does not stick to the steel, that is the correct temperature to take the blade out and quickly place it into the oil in the roasting pan. Practice a couple of times with this scrap piece of steel, getting it to the right temperature, so you learn the correct color.

Place your knife into the fire and bring it up to temperature. Quench it in your now-warm vegetable oil. Submerge the blade and let it cool for a couple of minutes. The clay will fall off, or you can scrape it off with a wooden stick.

Clean the blade with soap and water and then place it into the toaster oven. Set the temperature to 380 degrees Fahrenheit (no need to preheat the oven). Bake it for 1 hour. Turn off the toaster oven, open the door and let it cool. We call this step "tempering the blade."

No Warpage

Once cool, look down the length of the blade from the tip to see if it is straight. You can also place the blade on a flat surface and see if it rocks. If it did warp, you can secure the blade lengthwise to a piece of straight steel using metal clamps and put it back into the toaster at 350 degrees for another hour.

You can now sand the blade. Clean it with sandpaper using a foot-long, 1 ¼-inch-wide sanding block. I cut strips of sandpaper and hold them on the flat block to sand.

For this project, I started with 180-grit sandpaper and graduated up to an 800-grit abrasive block. I hand sanded the blade, which I clamped to a piece of 2-inch angle iron held in a vise.

You can clamp the knife on a bench and let the edge or point overhang, but this is dangerous. Bringing the blade point right up to the corner of the bench and clamping it provides a safe area to sand. My point is, you do not want a 6-inch pointed blade that you can accidentally bump into overhanging a bench.

With the blade polished to an appealing finish, you should be able to see the temper line. The hard edge will be brighter than the soft back. To make the temper line "pop," use diluted ferric chloride to lightly etch the blade (1 part chloride to 4 parts distilled water). You can also rub hot lemon juice onto the blade to make the temper line pop. After a 15-second etch, spray the blade with Windex to neutralize the ferric chloride. Then dry and spray with WD-40.

Next, place the blade on a paper towel on the bench and polish the oxide off with Peek polishing compound. You can use the Peek polish over the lemon juice. Oil the blade, wrap it in a paper towel and then tape it, so it stays wrapped, leaving only the handle exposed.

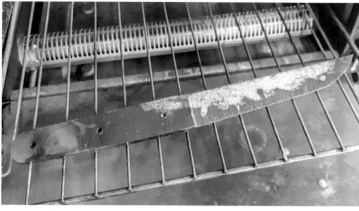

Place the blade into a toaster oven after quenching it in oil.

Glue & Pin Handle

Again, you can use whatever material you have for the handle slabs. I just wanted to demonstrate why wenge wood is cool, and it is a nod to my mentor, Don Fogg, who loved it. To glue the slabs onto the handle tang, I used J-B Weld Kwik. It is like a five-minute epoxy, but better. Glue on one handle slab, then drill out the wood from the other bare metal side. Glue on the second side and drill back through.

Please clamp the knife when drilling and be careful. You can shape the handle with a rasp, a sander, or sandpaper. A lot of new makers start fashioning knives with oversized boxy handles. Be mindful of this and think "chef's knife."

Glue the three pins in with the J-B Weld Kwik five-minute epoxy and file them flush with the outer face of the handle. Now you can use a wire wheel or wire brush to texture the handle.

With the blade done, this is the time you sharpen it. Use whatever stones you have, being careful not to scratch the sides of your knife.

I hope this helps you get started in knife making, and please be careful! □

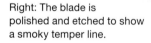

Right: The blade is polished and etched to show a smoky temper line.

Below: You can make a knife, like the finished tanto shown, this weekend.

TRENDS

They say you should collect the knives you like and not worry about whether they will increase in value for years to come. Perhaps that is because it is nearly impossible to predict which knives will become popular in the near or far future.

Prognosticators have their work cut out for them when it comes to handmade knives. Certain makers seemingly draw crowds immediately after setting their first knives on a show table. Others take years to gain a following and some never do.

Often the newest innovations, knifemaking materials, steels, and mechanisms never find adherents, regardless of how utilitarian or aesthetically superior they are. Other trends and state-of-the-art advances in technology and knife wizardry take off like rocket ships hellbent on the moon and beyond. Finally, there are patterns, styles, and models that disappear from the radar only to return with a vengeance. In the latter category, you can find the full-blown integrals, multi-blades, and coffin-handle bowies herein.

Of cutting-edge style and innovation are "The Resin-ators," "Raised-Clip Choppers," and knives in the Upscale Chef's Knives, Interesting Tactics, and Straight Razor Renaissance subdivisions of the Trends section. All are well-made, finely fit and finished examples of their kind, and they are so fun to look at and admire. Enjoy!

Coffin-Handle Bowies

It is such a cool knife handle style because of the imagery it conjures up—those old coffins standing against weathered facades of Western buildings awaiting burial without fanfare. Upon seeing them in old Westerns and sepia-tone prints, you know there was a shootout, crooks, murderers, and thieves.

Combine coffin-style handles with American bowie knife patterns, and there is enough history to go around and then some. Col. James Bowie was as much a part of the frontier fabric as Daniel Boone, Billy the Kid, and Annie Oakley. And like such renowned characters, the fascination with coffin-handle bowies will likely never go out of style.

The nice thing is that there don't have to be wars, shootouts, standoffs, murders, or fights for makers to fashion coffin-handle bowies. Just some sturdy steel, a local smithy, and a few slabs of old oak or even pine will do, perhaps the stuff of which the box is made.

» MATT PARKINSON
Whether you like a damascus fixed bowie or a 1084 mono-steel pocket bowie, and a coffin-style curly maple or a stabilized maple crotch wood handle, the maker has the knife for you. *(SharpByCoop image)*

» STEVE AUVENSHINE
The classic gentleman's bowie is built from a 1095 blade, a coffin-style curly walnut handle, nickel silver guard, and domed pins.

(SharpByCoop image)

⌄ MATT ROBERTS
A 1084-and-15N20 damascus blade leads off the "Proof of Concept" bowie that terminates in a coffin-style curly Movingui (satinwood) handle.

(SharpByCoop image)

⌃ NICK BACHTEL
With forge-finished wrought iron fittings and polished nickel silver accents, the random-pattern damascus bowie sports the obligatory coffin-style desert ironwood handle. *(SharpByCoop image)*

⌃ MICHAEL MCCLURE
The aesthetic of a damascus clip-point fixed blade with a coffin-shaped mammoth ivory handle is pure traditional bowie.

(BladeGallery.com image)

Mammoth Moxie

My hope was, years ago, upon self-discovering the magnificent natural material called mammoth ivory, that it would never run out. I prayed that Inuit in Greenland, Canada, and Alaska would not only be indefinitely allowed to harvest mammoth tusks and molars pushing up through the permafrost but also that enough of the woolly beasts had left this world from the icy reaches for there to be an unending supply of the stuff.

I am not sure about an endless supply, but so far, materials handlers and suppliers with connections in the Last Frontier and other northern territories have not run out.

Like the hue of an icy glacier on a sunny afternoon, blue mammoth ivory is as brilliant as the knifemakers using it for handles and hilts. It is the deep-sea or Mediterranean blue that is so hard to capture with paints, pigments, and cameras. The green stuff is gorgeous, and that orange, well, you cannot replicate it.

Sometimes nature has the upper hand, a way of reminding humankind that we are merely visitors and cannot dictate or control what is inherent, beautiful, and unspoiled. Mother Nature is a fierce and fickle matron with, in this case, a kind of mammoth moxie.

《 TOBIN HILL
One whaler's knife washes ashore in raindrop damascus blade steel and mammoth ivory handle scales. *(Eric Eggly, PointSeven image)*

》 JOHN DAVIS
Starburst damascus and mammoth tooth make up the better part of a flipper folder featuring ball-bearing action.
(SharpByCoop image)

《 TREVOR BURGER
Someone planted a mammoth molar bolster between the Bohler M390 blade and carbon fiber handle scales of a locking-liner folder.
(BladeGallery.com image)

» SHANE TAYLOR
Carved wooly mammoth ivory adds more depth to an already complex composite damascus folder with "radial W's"-pattern bolsters.
(BladeGallery.com image)

« STANLEY BUZEK
The blue-green mammoth ivory is a dealmaker for sure, with the damascus blade and acorn shield sweetening the pot.
(Caleb Royer image)

⌄ CHUCK GEDRAITIS
Blue-green mammoth ivory handle scales enliven the dress automatic folder featuring a Devin Thomas basketweave-pattern damascus blade, zirconium bolsters, and a titanium spacer, spring and liners.
(SharpByCoop image)

« JIM POOR
A fantastic fixed-blade fighter showcases a twist-pattern damascus blade, 1080 high carbon steel guard, and a highly figured mammoth ivory handle.
(SharpByCoop image)

⌃ DON HANSON III
It is amazing how alive ancient mammoth ivory can look on a W2 Fat Penny Trapper.
(SharpByCoop image)

« TOM PLOPPERT
With the handle large enough to do it justice, mammoth ivory is drop-dead gorgeous on a two-blade CPM-154 rope knife. *(Mitchell D. Cohen Photography)*

» JARRED BALL
Mammoth tusk and bog oak make up the handle half of a hand-forged model in a W2 blade with wild hamon (temper line). *(Caleb Royer image)*

« MICHAEL MCCLURE
A mammoth ivory-handle bowie features a long, slender damascus clip-point blade and oval stainless guard.
(BladeGallery.com image)

» JERRY HOSSOM
Matching an HHH Predator damascus blade with a mammoth ivory handle was a stroke of genius. *(Mitchell D. Cohen Photography)*

« CARL COLSON
It might be a CPM-154 whitetail hunter, but the handle is all woolly mammoth.
(SharpByCoop image)

⌃ JIM PROVOST
One of the most handsome drop-point hunters to come along, this one boasts a CPM-154 blade, mammoth molar handle, and a 416 stainless guard.
(SharpByCoop image)

⌃ IAN ROGERS
Mammoth tooth inlays in the amboyna burl handle of a full-tang, integral damascus Gyuto chef's knife add flavor to the recipe.
(Eric Eggly, PointSeven image)

« TIM ROBERTSON
The damascus blades are tightly patterned, the bark mammoth ivory handle scales highly figured, and the knife finely fit and finished
(SharpByCoop image)

》DES HORN
Rarely does one see mammoth ivory and meteorite combined for the handle and bolsters of a Damasteel folder, or maybe I just don't get out enough. *(BladeGallery.com image)*

《 JERRY MCCLURE
Gold inlay and engraving by Philip Kiesner bookend the green fossil mammoth ivory handle scales of a dress locking folder in a Chad Nichols stainless damascus blade. *(SharpByCoop image)*

《 REX MARSHALL
Equal parts impressive are the 10-inch, file-worked, 360-layer damascus blade, mammoth ivory handle and forged guard. *(Eric Eggly, PointSeven image)*

☙ RODRIGO ENGLERT
Possibly the luckiest integral gaucho knife in the world, it sashays a twist-damascus blade and fossil mammoth molar handle. *(Caleb Royer image)*

≋ KELLY VERMEER-VELLA
Feather damascus and mammoth ivory make for a powerful pairing on an S-guard bowie. *(Eric Eggly, PointSeven image)*

》RAPHAEL DURAND
Named the "Special Boxer," the semi-hollow ground damascus folder with mammoth ivory handle slabs is a knockout. *(SharpByCoop image)*

《 BILL RUPLE
It's pretty savage when you decorate a CPM-154 "Ax Handle" slip-joint folder with mammoth ivory, file work and engraving. *(SharpByCoop image)*

» JOHN APRIL
Blue mammoth ivory adds color and class to the hollow-ground, satin-finished CPM-154 fighter with a stainless guard, red G-10 liners and domed pins. *(SharpByCoop image)*

« PAUL SAVAGE
A D-guard bowie/fighter is outfitted in a 12-inch damascus blade with a pronounced clip and a mammoth ivory handle. *(Eric Eggly, PointSeven image)*

» BRETT NOAKE
When blue mammoth ivory is added into the mix, a damascus hunter takes on a whole new identity. *(Eric Eggly, PointSeven image)*

« RUSTY WAIDE
Yes, that's a blue mammoth ivory handle, one that looks painted with watercolors, on a damascus dress locking folder. *(SharpByCoop image)*

⌃ MIKE TYRE
Blue mammoth ivory and serpentine feather damascus add the crackle and pop to a bowie/fighter. *(SharpByCoop image)*

» GEORGE MULLER
All other woolly beasts were jealous when they saw the stabilized mammoth tooth used for the handle of a hollow-ground flipper folder, this in a "Grosse Rosen"-pattern Damasteel blade and Gibeon meteorite bolsters. *(BladeGallery.com image)*

⌃ RICHARD S. WRIGHT
Mammoth ivory handle scales are the perfect counterpart to a J.D. Smith "Crushed W's"-pattern damascus blade, random-pattern bolsters and forged-to-shape cross guards. A 1.25-ounce sterling silver knife fob is sculpted into the likeness of Bill McHenry as a tribute to the knifemaker and teacher.

KENDALL SCHORSCH
I mean, in addition to the clean fit and finish of the CPM-154 blades and stainless bolsters and frame, and some incredible scalloped file work, the mammoth ivory just makes the piece.
(SharpByCoop image)

BRIAN MILINSKI
An Alabama damascus hunter is handled in blue-dyed, crosscut fossilized mammoth ivory secured with mosaic pins. *(Caleb Royer image)*

SAM UKEILEY
A "Burly Gent" hits the town in a bold feather-damascus blade, mammoth ivory handle scales, and brass-infused carbon fiber bolsters.
(SharpByCoop image)

DENNIS FRIEDLY
A CPM-154 gent's bowie benefits from mammoth ivory handle scales and gold inlay and engraving by Joe Mason.
(SharpByCoop image)

KIRK REXROAT
With more than just blue mammoth ivory moxie, the small folder showcases two-tone anodized titanium, Mokumé bolsters and a damascus blade.
(Eric Eggly, PointSeven image)

ARTHUR WASHBURN
A "Small Saber Tooth" looks resplendent in a raindrop-pattern Devin Thomas damascus blade, a mammoth ivory handle, and Mokumé gane bolsters.
(BladeGallery.com image)

PAUL LUSK
Get a load of those chompers—the AEB-L fixed blades and the mammoth ivory handles.
(SharpByCoop image)

Straight Razor
Renaissance

The renaissance is not as much a revival of straight razors as it is a reimagining of everything collectors, makers, and enthusiasts thought the pattern was and could be. These are not traditionally styled razors that have lain beside mugs and brushes in barbershops for centuries. No, the custom pieces herein elevate the genre to new levels.

Between file-worked spines that resemble dragon tales and scales to damascus blades, carbon fiber bolsters and composite handles, the straight razors arrive ready to shave yet most likely destined for the display cabinet. They are as pretty to look at as they are capable of shaving whiskers after a few strokes on a stone and strop.

Definitely a trend-turned-fixture in the handmade knife industry, the straight razor renaissance reawakens a classic edged tool design, one meant to be used and admired. It has succeeded in that respect.

» STUART KERR
The "Dragon Spine" razor relies on a Bruce Barnett "River of Fire" damascus blade and a "Red Dark Matter" carbon composite handle.
(SharpByCoop image)

» ALEX JACQUES
For the Tao straight razor, a Wootz damascus blade forged by Evrahim Baran and a sculpted copper, brass and G-10 handle go hand in hand. The razor features symbols and Chinese characters from the Taoist Bagua representing north, south, east and west.

(SharpByCoop image)

« MARDI MESHEJIAN
Drawing inspiration from European straight razors, the maker forged a "Twisted W's" damascus blade for the piece, sculpted superconductor bolsters and inlaid mammoth ivory for the handle. *(BladeGallery.com image)*

⌃ STEPHAN and ADRIAN VAN DEVENTER
A V-Toku2 carbon steel blade slides silently out from a stabilized box elder burl handle with lightning strike carbon fiber bolsters.

(BladeGallery.com image)

Spike in
Stabilized and Spalted
Maple

Like a nice, traditional walnut rifle stock, with maybe a little checkering thrown in and some steel, gold, silver or pewter inlays, spalted and stabilized maple burl knife handles bespeak sophistication and historical significance.

"Mesmerizing" is such an overused word, but you certainly can get lost in the grains and swirls of highly figured maple burl. Heck, give it a whirl—it is OK to take time to appreciate what Mother Nature has brought forth. The lively handle material is pleasing to the senses, provides stability to knives and feels good in the grip.

Knifemakers obviously value maple burl and get the material stabilized from suppliers for the grips of their blades. There has been a spike in the number of maple burl handle custom knives of late, perhaps because craftsmen and collectors know a good thing when they see it and appreciate the material for what it is.

« STEVE THOMPSON
Dyed maple burl will make the mouth water, and the 1084-and-15N20 damascus blade with nickel silver guard and copper spacers is a tasty combo.
(SharpByCoop image)

JOHN APRIL
Curly maple adds a splash of color to a 1075 tanto with brass, nickel silver, and buffalo horn accents.
(SharpByCoop image)

DAVID KELLEY
A particularly spectacular spalted maple handle makes an appearance on an O1 hunter with thumb notches and tapered tang.
(Eric Eggly, PointSeven image)

JESSE PROFFITT
The hammer-forged 1095 beauty displays a smoky hamon (temper line), stabilized curly maple grip, denim Micarta spacer, brass pins and white G-10 liners.
(Caleb Royer image)

DIONATAM FRANCO
A hunter orchestrated in Turkish twist damascus and stabilized maple burl comes in a tooled black leather sheath. *(BladeGallery. com image)*

» MATT PARKINSON
Highly figured spalted maple and incredibly patterned "Bjorkmans Twist" Damasteel vie for attention in the confines of a modern chef's knife.
(SharpByCoop image)

» CHRIS SHIRES
Stabilized maple burl looks sticky sweet on an AEB-L stainless chef's knife with Macassar ebony bolsters.
(BladeGallery.com image)

« C. LUIS PINA
An integral damascus Gokujo boning knife showcases an upswept blade, integral bolster and red dyed maple burl handle.
(BladeGallery.com image)

« JIM POLING
The forged 5160 fixed blade boasts a Parkerized mild steel hilt, copper spacer, domed nickel silver pin and stabilized maple burl handle.
(Caleb Royer image)

⌄ SASHA ROSENFELD
You won't misplace the stabilized maple burl-handled 1084 chef's knife in the kitchen. *(BladeGallery.com image)*

⌃ DAN BIDINGER
The stabilized maple burl handle scales of an AEB-L stainless chef's knife are set off by black paper Micarta liners.
(BladeGallery.com image)

《 DAN TOMPKINS
A spectacular clip-point chef's knife is done up in a 52100 blade and a dyed and stabilized curly maple handle with brass perimeter pins. The bolster is bog oak, and the finish on the blade is an orange peel patina.
(Caleb Royer image)

》 JARED LEES
Call it a fusion hunter/chef's knife executed in W2 tool steel, maple burl, white G-10 and vintage brown paper Micarta.
(Caleb Royer image)

⩔ AN
Spalted
G-10 han
stainless fli
up a bit. (Blade

》 JESSE HU

Sporting a semi-chaotic hamon (temper line), the K-tip Gyuto pattern chef's knife is done up in a 1095 blade and a stabilized maple burl handle.

(Caleb Royer image)

《 KENNETH WEBB

A stabilized and spalted maple burl handle has as much character as the 1084-and-15N20 mosaic damascus blade of the fighter, both highlighted by nickel silver and Mokumé gane spacers.

(SharpByCoop image)

》 ADAM MILLE

The fighter hits the ring in a differentially tempered 1084 high-carbon steel blade and a quilted maple handle.

(SharpByCoop image)

DRE THORBURN
maple inlays within the black
le frame of a CTS-XHP
per folder spice things
Gallery.com image)

» JEFF FARIA
A-hunting it goes, in an O-1 tool steel blade, dyed and stabilized maple handle and stainless guard.
(Caleb Royer image)

» DAVID HALL
Between the flat-ground Nitro V stainless blade and the green quilted maple handle is a stainless guard and some black G-10 spacers.
(Caleb Royer image)

» WARREN WALL
Handsome is the dyed and stabilized maple burl handle of the Santoku chef's knife, accented by Bocote and butted up against a hand-forged damascus blade.
(BladeGallery.com image)

Well-Honed Hunters

« CARL COLSON
After downing the monster buck, he coaxed the Alabama damascus hunter from its form-fitted leather sheath, curled his fingers around the amber stag grip and went to work field dressing the animal. *(SharpByCoop image)*

» BOB APPLEBY
In the well-honed hunter realm comes an AEB-L drop-point fixed blade featuring an amber-dyed crown stag handle. *(SharpByCoop image)*

⌃ DON HANSON III
A full-tang clip-point hunter is orchestrated via carbon steel recovered from an antique sawmill blade and stabilized Missouri black walnut. *(BladeGallery.com image)*

« JIM PROVOST
The eye bounces back and forth between the "Odin's Eye" Damacore blade and the stabilized cedar burl handle of the drop-point hunter. *(SharpByCoop image)*

« DENNIS FRIEDLY
The "Africa" Pro Hunter is a CPM-154 beauty in a mammoth ivory handle and stainless bolsters engraved by Gil Rudolph. *(SharpByCoop image)*

» BILL BEHNKE
The 1084-and-15N20 damascus hunter is handled in walnut and stag with black and yellow spacers.
(Eric Eggly, PointSeven image)

» KEVIN HARVEY
Amenities of a harpoon-point hunter/camp knife include a ladder-pattern damascus blade, engraved nickel silver guard and Australian ringed Gidgee handle. *(BladeGallery.com image)*

RONNIE SMITH
The W2 raised-clip hunter stalks its prey in stabilized quilted maple and curly oak.
(Caleb Royer image)

MATT BAILEY
A harpoon-tip utility/hunting knife features a full-tang, hand-forged san mai blade, an ironwood handle and a mosaic pin.
(BladeGallery.com image)

ROBERT ERICKSON
A Persian-style hunter relies on a CPM-S45VN blade, bronze guard, and a stabilized curly Koa handle.
(SharpByCoop image)

DON FOGG
A forge-finished tool steel blade was the right choice for the stag-handle hunter.
(SharpByCoop image)

BOB LAY
A Canadian drop-point hunter is fashioned from CPM-154 stainless steel, brass fittings, a cocobolo handle and one sheep horn spacer. *(BladeGallery.com image)*

KENT CARTER
The clean drop-point hunter is held fast by stag handle scales and stainless bolts, and features a nicely engraved guard. *(Eric Eggly, PointSeven image)*

DAVID DAVIS
One big bowie-style, hidden-tang Alabama damascus hunter dresses the part in stabilized buckeye burl, ebony, bone and nickel silver.

(Caleb Royer image)

RICARDO VILAR
There's always room in the pack for a starburst-damascus clip-point hunter with an ancient walrus ivory handle. *(BladeGallery.com image)*

BRETT NOAKE

Cut from chevron-pattern damascus and curly Koa, the hunting knife is of the high-quality kind. *(Eric Eggly, PointSeven image)*

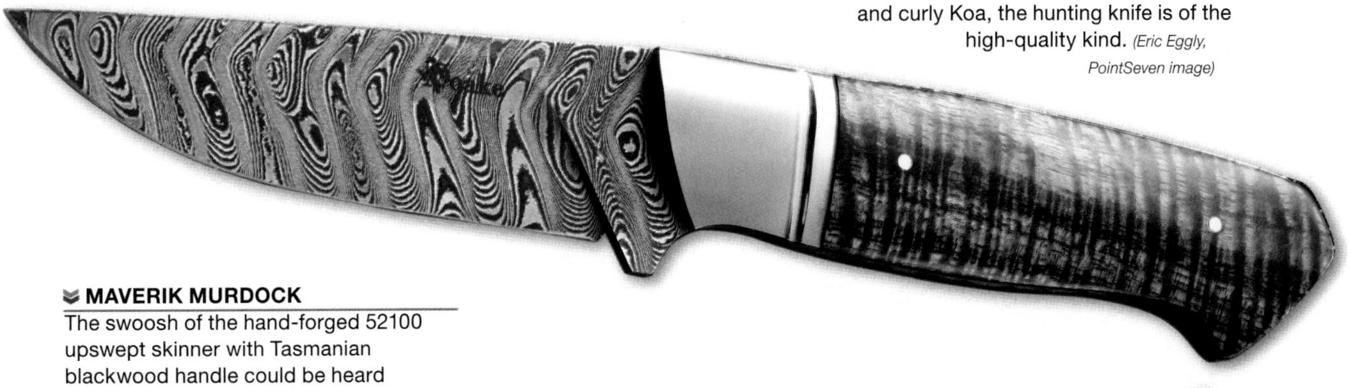

MAVERIK MURDOCK

The swoosh of the hand-forged 52100 upswept skinner with Tasmanian blackwood handle could be heard throughout the forest. *(BladeGallery.com image)*

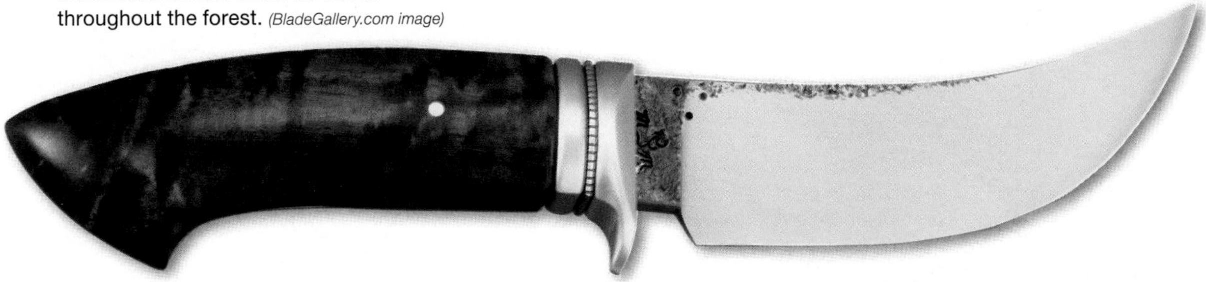

BILL BURKE

Only ironwood and brass would do for the traditional, finely fit and finished drop-point hunter.

(BladeGallery.com image)

ANDREW FRANKLAND

One 4-inch drop-point hunter with some wood grains and file work along the blade spine is all one needs to start the day.

AARON LAWVERE

A gentleman's skinner is executed in a CPM-S30V blade, dovetailed nickel silver bolsters and desert ironwood handle scales.

(SharpByCoop image)

TOM PLOPPERT
A CPM-440V hunting knife set made for Zac Brown, the pre-ban elephant ivory handles are engraved by Joe Mason, and the Larry Parsons sheath includes a concho fashioned by Rick Dunkerley.
(SharpByCoop image)

JASON CLARK
The Damasteel "Mini Hunter" is a locking-liner folder featuring marble carbon fiber handle scales and heat-colored and polished zirconium bolsters.
(BladeGallery.com image)

ANDY ISAACKS
A drop-point hunter with a full, tapered tang and a leather thong gets the green-dyed burl handle treatment. *(Eric Eggly, PointSeven image)*

JACCO VAN DE BRUINHORST
The European hunter parades a "Fireblast" damascus blade, presentation-grade desert ironwood handle and Gabon ebony spacers.
(Caleb Royer image)

BENJAMIN WHITAKER
Desert ironwood pulls duty on a wave-pattern Alabama damascus hunter. *(Caleb Royer image)*

⌃ **MIKE CLARK**
Amboyna burl is paired with 15N20 and 1084 damascus for the sporty drop-point hunter. *(BladeGallery.com image)*

⌃ **ROBERT CROWDER**
With a desert ironwood handle like that, one would be advised to fashion a drop-point hunter featuring a twist-pattern damascus blade and a Mokumé gane guard. *(BladeGallery. com image)*

⌃ **JEREMY BARTLETT**
With a san mai blade and buckeye burl handle, the drop-point hunter has character to spare. *(Eric Eggly, PointSeven image)*

⌃ **KYLE HANSON**
There's a reason why fixed-blade drop-point hunters with green canvas Micarta handles and smoky temper lines haven't fallen out of favor.

(SharpByCoop image)

⌃ **DAVID KELLEY**
This is the way you want to see O1 drop-point hunters—highly fit and finished, including stag grips, stainless guards, and red and black spacers. *(Caleb Royer image)*

⌄ GREGER FORSELIUS

The Swedish long hunter relies on a forged-to-shape damascus blade and a contoured Arizona desert ironwood and birch handle.

(BladeGallery.com image)

⌄ RICH RICHARDSON

Engraved scrollwork and copper liners, spacer, and bolts highlight the drop point hunter incorporating a Devin Thomas damascus blade, camel bone handle and ebony bolsters. *(Caleb Royer image)*

⌃ KURT SWEARINGEN

Taking out this Buffalo Hunter set in CPM 154 blade steel and stabilized black ash burl handles is like bringing out the fine china on Christmas. *(SharpByCoop image)*

⌞ MICHAEL MCCLURE

The hunting tradition comes alive through the 1084 carbon steel fixed blade handled in stag, stacked leather, and stainless.

(BladeGallery.com image)

» J. ALEX RUIZ

In a nod to one of the greats, Alex fashions a Bob Loveless style "Piker" in a 1084 blade and a stabilized pomelle bubinga handle.

(Caleb Royer image)

⌄ TELL DEATRICH
If you're going to build a hunting knife set, you might as well use 52100 ball-bearing steel and some burnt orange synthetic handles. *(Caleb Royer image)*

⌄ JIM COFFEE
The 1084-and-15N20 damascus clip-point hunter sports a sambar stag handle and blued steel fittings. *(Eric Eggly, PointSeven image)*

« TOMMY GANN
Sometimes, all you need to pursue happiness is a thumbprint damascus hunter with an amber-jigged bone handle. *(BladeGallery.com image)*

⌃ JOSE SANTIAGO CUMMINGS
A clean, recurved CPM 154 drop-point hunter is guarded and handled in buffalo horn, abalone shell, resin, G-10 and Bolivian rosewood. The blade also features abalone shell inlays and rope file work. *(Caleb Royer image)*

⌃ EDDIE STALCUP
The maker outdid himself with those waterbuck horn handle scales on a file-worked, 9-inch, flat-back CTS-XHP hunter.

» MARC ALDRICH
With a Nessmuk-style AEB-L blade, the hunter enters the fray in a stabilized lace redwood handle, a stainless and copper guard, and a domed copper pin.
(SharpByCoop image)

» ERIK MCCRIGHT
Any hunter would like to bag the twist-damascus fixed blade in a heat-colored collar and frame, stag handle, nickel silver liner, and spacer. *(Caleb Royer image)*

» DIONATAM FRANCO
A colossally cool, clean Turkish twist damascus hunter with matching guard and pommel is adorned with a stabilized amboyna burl handle.
(BladeGallery.com image)

⌃ SIMON RHODES
A traditional fixed blade hunter is executed in 1084-and-15N20 damascus, a mild steel guard, walnut handle and brass and G-10 fittings. *(SharpByCoop image)*

« JAMES WHITE
Reserving Brazilian cherrywood for just such an occasion, the maker forged a 1084 hunter with a stainless guard and musk ox and brass spacers.
(SharpByCoop image)

Centuries of
Swords

» J. BRENT SMITH
The 21-inch blade of
the hunting sword is a
four-bar stack, 92 layers
each, of 1084-and-15N20
damascus accompanied
by a Tasmanian blackwood
hilt with mother-of-pearl
and black-lip pearl spacers.
(SharpByCoop image)

« SAM TAYLOR
The "Silver Ghost" haunts its
victims via a 37-inch forged
titanium-niobium blade, cast
sterling silver guard engraved
with Chinese characters
meaning "Silver Ghost,"
and a stacked leather grip.
(SharpByCoop image)

》VINCE EVANS
As if a gilt bronze and silver guard and pommel were not enough, the Danish ring-hilt sword features a four-bar composite herringbone damascus blade and a stabilized black ash hilt. The piece is inspired by an original 7th-century sword found in Kyndby, Denmark.

(SharpByCoop image)

《 GARY HOUSE
At 38 inches overall, the 1084-and-15N20 damascus doozy dons a grooved tiger maple hilt.

(Eric Eggly, PointSeven image)

《 PETER MARTIN
Making the sign of the cross might not be a bad idea when chancing upon the 80CrV2 Templar's Sword in a leather-wrapped wooden hilt.

(Cory Martin Imaging)

» MATTHEW BERRY
Modeled beautifully after a 15th-century Bastard Sword, the maker's version combines an 80CRV2 blade with a wrought iron guard, leather handle and hollow-cast bronze pommel.

(SharpByCoop image)

« MATT PARKINSON
A ring-hilt sword stands tall in a 35-inch L6 blade and a leather-wrapped poplar hilt.

(SharpByCoop image)

« JUSTIN BURTON
A modern twist on a katana involves 120-layer damascus, a carbon fiber handle, counter-sunk brass bolts and a hammered brass guard. *(Caleb Royer image)*

Raised-Clip
Choppers

A h, those raised clips! Other than a true knife enthusiast, no one on God's green Earth would know what someone was talking about when referring to a raised clip—the blade's spine on bowie-like knives and other choppers that juts up abruptly before tapering back down toward the point.

Bowies have always had clip points, perhaps becoming more pronounced over the years. Recently, an increasing number of knifemakers have started designing some models with more prominently raised clips.

After all, if something has inherently sexy lines, why not accentuate them?

Those sexy lines sure do look good on big old choppers and recurved bowies. It is not enough that the wide, beefy blades are the center of attention in the first place. Now their designers are enhancing the patterns and doing what knifemakers do—overbuilding the pieces.

That is not a bad thing. After all, who doesn't love a big, beefy raised-clip chopper?

» JARED LEES
The blade of the Santoku, complete with raised clip—in this case for chopping—is Dion Damascus CuMail steel—and accompanied by ringed Gidgee wood, no less.
(*Caleb Royer image*)

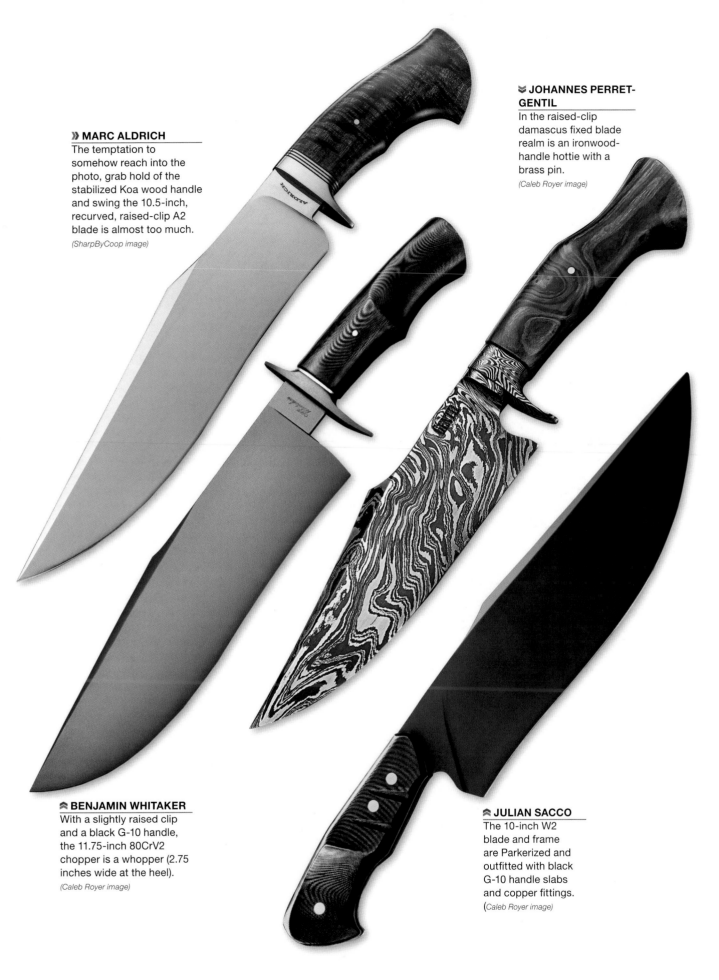

» MARC ALDRICH
The temptation to somehow reach into the photo, grab hold of the stabilized Koa wood handle and swing the 10.5-inch, recurved, raised-clip A2 blade is almost too much.

(SharpByCoop image)

⌄ JOHANNES PERRET-GENTIL
In the raised-clip damascus fixed blade realm is an ironwood-handle hottie with a brass pin.

(Caleb Royer image)

⌃ BENJAMIN WHITAKER
With a slightly raised clip and a black G-10 handle, the 11.75-inch 80CrV2 chopper is a whopper (2.75 inches wide at the heel).

(Caleb Royer image)

⌃ JULIAN SACCO
The 10-inch W2 blade and frame are Parkerized and outfitted with black G-10 handle slabs and copper fittings.

(Caleb Royer image)

» JARRED BALL
At 15 inches overall, the recurved W2 fixed blade has a pronounced hamon (temper line) and a stabilized spalted tamarind grip.
(Caleb Royer image)

JORDON BERTHELOT
The bolo/kukri showcases a sculpted Justin Reynolds san mai damascus blade with a slightly raised clip, a Mokume guard and a black California buckeye burl handle. *(Caleb Royer image)*

« JUSTIN BURTON
The "PWENT" Dwarven-inspired chopper is forged from 1970's-era leaf springs and finished with an acid stonewash.
(Caleb Royer image)

» ROBERT ERICKSON
The curly Koa-bodied "Terosaur" lashes out with its 6-inch Vanadis 4e fang.
(SharpByCoop image)

« CLAUDIO and ARIEL SOBRAL (CAS Brothers)
Acting as a stinger on the stag-handle "Scorpion" is a hand-forged K720 carbon steel blade with a mustard patina.
(BladeGallery.com image)

» JEREMY YELLE
The 5160 integral with raised clip needs nothing more than an ironwood handle attached via domed pin.
(Caleb Royer image)

⌄ DYLAN BRUGMAN
The maker's first attempt at a frame-handle sub-hilt fixed blade resulted in a wicked raised-clip chopper.
(Caleb Royer image)

⌃ JASON FRY
A sub-hilt fighter, he goes by the name "El Diablo," wearing a "trash can" canister damascus blade forged from damascus scraps and 1095 powder, and a ringed Gidgee handle.
(SharpByCoop image)

« ZAC CAMACHO
Featuring a 42-layer damascus blade in a harpoon tip, the edged artwork comes in a black canvas Micarta, brass and stabilized bog oak handle.
(Caleb Royer image)

Upscale Chef's Knives

C hef's knives are the hottest thing going in the industry. Sounds like a bold statement, doesn't it? A short two years ago, that designation would have been reserved for flipper folders, particularly those fashioned using exotic materials like Timascus, Moku-Ti, CarboQuartz, G-Tec, zirconium and lightning strike carbon fiber.

Chef's knives have been gaining adherents and notoriety for the past few years and have hit their peak. The trend started with cooking shows like "Top Chef" and "Chopped" on the Food Network. And it was bolstered by the "Buy Local" and self-sufficient living movements and then propelled further forward by the worldwide pandemic that saw people working from home and preparing more meals in the kitchen.

It is amazing how useful a quality chef's knife is in the kitchen when your stomach is growling and the kids need to be fed. Paring knives are just not good veggie choppers.

The upscale chef's knives on this and the following pages would be the stars of the kitchen, regardless of whether Bobby Flay was in the house.

《 DERICK KEMPER

In a san mai blade of damascus with a W2 core, the chef's knife cuts the mustard alright, while holding the Hornbeam handle, of course.

(SharpByCoop image)

MACKENZIE ARRINGTON
Welcome to "Primetime"— one of a three-piece kitchen knife set in 15N20 high carbon steel and a black and gold Trustone, yellow brass, and G-10 handle. (*SharpByCoop image*)

DAN BIDINGER
The cocobolo, paper Micarta and G-10 handle of the AEB-L chef's knife looks fantastic protruding from the butcher block.
(*Eric Eggly, PointSeven image*)

MATTHEW PARKINSON
The serrated or scalloped edge of the Damasteel bread knife was not done with a machine, nor was the stabilized blond Koa handle automatically made.
(*SharpByCoop image*)

BRIAN TIGHE
The Damasteel Gyuto chef's knife is handled in "brain coral carbon fiber" with a brass-infused carbon fiber spacer.
(*BladeGallery.com image*)

SASHA ROSENFELD
The 11.25-inch hand-forged damascus blade should slice through the ham, roast or sushi rolls with ease, handled in stabilized ancient bog oak with lace redwood spacers.
(*BladeGallery.com image*)

DAN TOMPKINS
A modern evolution in cutlery involves such features as Japanese Blue #2 san mai steel, spalted birch handles, G-10 bolsters, and redwood and box elder burl spacers.
(*Caleb Royer image*)

« BRANDON HAMPTON
For the southpaws, the "Left-Handed Takohiki" sushi knife is built with an SM100 hardened titanium blade, a Honduran rosewood handle and G-10 liners. *(SharpByCoop image)*

» ALEX HOSSOM
The pride of any kitchen, the cutlery set features CTS-XHP blades and Koa wood handles.
(Mitchell D. Cohen Photography)

» JELLE HAZENBERG
Upscale features of a 9-inch chef's knife include a hand-forged 26c3 blade with clay-quench hamon and a sculpted two-tone ebony handle. *(Caleb Royer image)*

« WILLIAM KALKBRENNER
The high-performance Honyaki Sujihiki slicing knife showcases a long, slender W2 blade with a Japanese clay zone hamon (temper line), an antiqued copper bolster and a black ash burl handle. *(BladeGallery.com image)*

» JASON ELLARD
Not your average kitchen slicer, the twisted mosaic damascus blade gets a ringed Gidgee handle, domed pin and mirror-polished stainless and basketweave mosaic damascus spacers.

(SharpByCoop image)

⌃ WARREN WALL
As pretty while slicing ham as it is eggplant, the integral damascus chef's knife is dressed in purple dyed and stabilized curly maple.
(BladeGallery.com image)

⌄ JAMES ARBUCKLE
Not an upscale chef's knife? Tell that to the gourmet cook who needs an AEB-L meat cleaver with a purpleheart handle. *(BladeGallery.com image)*

》 ISAIAH SCHROEDER
The "Skeleton" Nakiri-style chef's knife showcases a powdered steel blade with a nickel skeleton lying on its side and right on top of the 1084 cutting bar that was forge-welded on. The piece also sports a hexagonal African blackwood handle.

(Cory Martin Imaging)

⌃ DAVID TUTHILL
An instant classic, the prettily patterned damascus chef's knife comes in a big leaf maple burl handle with silicon bronze and vulcanized paper spacers. *(Eric Eggly, PointSeven image)*

⌄ AIDAN GARRITY
A "K Tip Kitchen Knife" dons a 1095-and-15N20 damascus blade, copper bolster and a black linen Micarta handle.

(SharpByCoop image)

》 DAVID LISCH
Walnut gets co-billing alongside a forged-to-shape "Wolf Pack" mosaic damascus blade with integral bolster.

(BladeGallery.com image)

《 RICARDO VILAR
In the dyed and stabilized maple and ladder-pattern damascus realm, complete with integral bolster, the chef's knife is ready to hit the cutting board.

(BladeGallery.com image)

BILL BURKE
Atypical as far as paring knives go, the utility tool of the kitchen shows off a hand-forged damascus blade and integral bolster and a stabilized, presentation-grade Tasmanian blackwood handle. *(BladeGallery.com image)*

JERRY GOETTIG
If one feels particularly patriotic in the kitchen, the maker fashions a satin-finished AEB-L stainless chef's knife in a "We the People" paper Micarta handle. *(BladeGallery.com image)*

JEREMY BARTLETT
A 1095 Gyuto-style chef's knife is served up with tasty sides of imitation ivory and buckeye burl.

(Caleb Royer image)

ALLEN NEWBERRY
The broths might not be spoiled, but the chefs certainly are when considering knives like this one featuring a clay hardened W2 blade with wavy hamon and rosewood burl handle scales.

(Caleb Royer image)

JOSE SANTIAGO-CUMMINGS
The handle of the W2 cook's knife is a progression, starting nearest the blade, from mastodon ivory to buffalo horn with an abalone inlay, to a blue spacer, Bolivian rosewood, green spacer and mahogany burl.

(Caleb Royer image)

IAN ROGERS
One lucky chef will be preparing ingredients using a hand-forged damascus Gyuto in a stabilized Koa handle and a mammoth molar spacer.

(BladeGallery.com image)

⌄ ANDREA LISCH
With slicing and paring knife elements, the feather-pattern damascus fixed blade sports an Arizona desert ironwood handle. *(BladeGallery.com image)*

⌄ JORDAN LAMOTHE
In a "Brute de Forge" style, the chef's knife parades a hand-forged 80CrV2 blade, phenolic bolster, nickel silver spacer and a stabilized, spalted elm handle.

(BladeGallery.com image)

≫ JESS HOFFMAN
A "Cocaire" ("chef" in Gaelic) slicer integrates an Elmax blade and York gum burl handle.

(Cory Martin Imaging)

« TOM BUCKNER
One would be promoted from sous to executive chef just for walking into the kitchen with the Thor-pattern Damasteel knife with curly koa handle and sculpted bolster.

(SharpByCoop image)

⌄ EDWARD RATANUM
A W2 Nakiri chef's knife is treated to a stabilized amboyna burl handle with a single resin spacer.

(BladeGallery.com image)

≫ NICHOLAS ORR
Check out the black and white ebony handle on her, not to mention the 85-layer twist damascus blade, carbon fiber bolster and TruStone and G-10 spacers.

(Caleb Royer image)

GABRIEL MABRY
If wanting to hone one's skills in the kitchen, an excellent place to start would be using the integral Gyuto chef's knife with hand-forged damascus blade, and dyed and stabilized curly cottonwood handle. *(BladeGallery.com image)*

JORDON BERTHELOT
Deboning just became so much more interesting using a 6-inch chef's knife in a san mai blade of Chad Nichols stainless damascus over an XHP core, a Honduran rosewood grip from Scott Johns Scale Workz and stainless Corby bolts.
(Caleb Royer image)

ANDREW BURKE
Once you have acquired this damascus Gyuto, you'll want to grip the octagonal Macassar ebony handle and possibly not let go.
(BladeGallery.com image)

JONAS JOHNSSON
The Honyaki-style Japanese kitchen knife comes in a 26C3 steel blade with a curlicued hamon and a stacked birchbark handle.
(Caleb Royer image)

SCOTT FOX
The clouds and sky are represented within the 1095 steel blade and dyed box elder burl handle, complete with white G-10 liners, of an 8.5-inch chef's knife. *(Caleb Royer image)*

MARDI MESHEJIAN
Quilted cottonwood, hand-forged damascus and anodized titanium take turns on a damascus Gyuto chef's knife. *(BladeGallery.com image)*

JAMES OATLEY
A Chinese-style cleaver incorporates a forged Damasteel blade and a Fat Carbon composite carbon fiber handle.
(BladeGallery.com image)

DALE MILLER
Black and white ebony gives a 9 1/8-inch S-ground 52100 chef's knife its stripes.
(BladeGallery.com image)

IVAN BERLATZKY
If you color coordinate your kitchen cutlery, then this might be your lucky day. The 8-inch chef's knife with a patinated K110 steel blade and Grevillea wood handle goes with anything.
(Caleb Royer image)

MERT TANSU
Taking inspiration from Yatagan swords, Mert built a Wootz steel chef's knife in a walrus ivory handle and bronze bolster.
(Caleb Royer image)

RONNIE SMITH
Some lucky chef will be slicing roast beef with that 9-inch W2 blade, complete with cloudy hamon, and a black quilted maple handle, copper pins, and white G-10 bolster.
(Caleb Royer image)

NIKO NICOLAIDES
With a damascus blade forged from 1084 and 15N20 steels, the 5.75-inch chef's knife hits the butcher block in an integral bolster and desert ironwood handle.
(BladeGallery.com image)

JESSICA BURKE
A bold "twisted W's"-pattern damascus blade leads the way on a Macassar ebony-handle chef's knife with a buffalo horn ferrule.

(BladeGallery.com image)

MICHAEL ZIEBA and DALE CUCOS
Michael coached young maker Dale Cucos in finishing this Pro Chef's set, marked with both names and ground from "Thor"-pattern Damasteel blades.

(SharpByCoop image)

JACKSON RUMBLE
A European-style chef's knife gets the full hand-forged damascus and Camatillo (Mexican kingwood) treatment.

(BladeGallery.com image)

C. LUIS PINA
An integral mosaic damascus Sujihiki slicer is forged with an integral mustard-finished bolster and given a black ash burl handle.

(BladeGallery.com image)

KEITH BARTHELMES
The Western chef's knife was made for a local restaurant using AEB-L stainless steel and a beautiful piece of dyed big-leaf maple burl.

(Caleb Royer image)

JOHN PHILLIPS
A Nakiri chef's knife is prepared using a stainless Damasteel blade with deep fuller, a synthetic horn and brass bolster, and a Koa wood grip.

(SharpByCoop image)

The Resin-ators

Resins are everywhere now. They have made inroads in the form of curving, winding, stream-like formations carving through wood on coffee and end tables, filling in gaps, burly knots and voids along their way, highlighting natural grains and adding color.

The resins do not get there naturally, of course. Man adds them, enhancing the beauty of wood if that is possible. On knives, they look killer. Resins of all colors are brilliant additions to the handles, bolsters and pommels of custom blades and kitchen cutlery.

Often melted and poured in as if hot lead, molten lava or liquid gold and silver, the resins take their own routes. Rivers of scorching resins cut through the walls of knife materials, bed down and make their claims within the confines of knives.

Other times blocks of resins are simply cut, shaped and otherwise molded into bolsters or handles. Either way, it is a brilliant material, stable, hard, conforming and cool. Thank goodness for the resin-ators who breathe life into the substance and bring it to market.

« STUART KERR
Not your daddy's straight razor, the "Hexx Dragon" enlists a "River of Fire" damascus blade and a Hex Resin composite handle with a glass fiber liner.
(SharpByCoop image)

» THOMAS KILLINGSWORTH
"Clever Girl" is all gussied up in raindrop damascus, titanium and Juma Blue Snake (resin) scales. *(SharpByCoop image)*

« DES HORN
As if being a ball-release Damasteel gent's flipper folder with anodized titanium bolsters was n't enough, the piece features a Raffir composite aluminum-meshed handle in a translucent epoxy resin.

(BladeGallery.com image)

⌃ BRANDON HAMPTON
While the DLC-coated blade of the "Mioroshi Deba" sports a two-tone grind, the handle combines buckeye burl and resin.

(SharpByCoop image)

« MACKENZIE ARRINGTON
In addition to an etched 15N20 high carbon blade, the "Sprout" petty knife parades a stabilized madrone, cottonwood burl and dyed resin handle.

(SharpByCoop image)

GABRIEL MABRY
Between the "River Delta" damascus blade and the stabilized box elder burl handle of the chef's knife is synthetic resin and black G-10.

(BladeGallery.com image)

JESSE PROFFITT
The composite handle of the flat-ground and differentially hardened 1095 fixed blade is a composite of end-grain curly maple with purple/gold resin. *(Caleb Royer image)*

PETER PRUYN
The "Mill Ghost Tomahawk" is forged from a recycled sawmill blade, given a mosaic-damascus "a Skulla" bolster and hafted in Voodoo Resin by Matt Peterson.

(SharpByCoop image)

ALEXANDER NOOT
A materials amalgamation, the knife features an "explosion" damascus blade, Mokume guard, and a handle of contrasting stabilized Raffir wood (filled to the core with resin) slabs and ShockRes™ Alumilite urethane patterns.

(Caleb Royer image)

WES LYONS
Copper runs through the knife—in the CuMai blade of 15N20, copper and 80CrV2 steel, and within the J Hue Customs CopperCore hybrid handle scales of resin, copper and wood.

(Caleb Royer image)

Dressed for Success
Folders

I love it when knifemakers call them "Sunday go-to-meetin' knives," "dress folders," "fancy pieces," or "my dress-up knife." I mean, come on, that's so Andy Griffith to have a special, fancy knife for going into town, church on Sunday or dinner with that special someone.

It is more of a form-following-function thing, though. Most guys and gals who fashion folding knives also use them for chores. They work their knives, maintain them, hone the edges and respect the blades. Inevitably, the edges get nicks, the blades discolor, the handles wear, and the bolsters crack, dent or become damaged.

No self-respecting knifemaker pulls out a cattleman's knife with oil, dirt, grease or blood on the blade to slice a thread from his lovely's dress, to pry a paperclip from his boss's agenda or open a package during a family holiday.

No, these are "Dressed for Success Folders," a bit of elegance in a busy workingperson's life. They will cut with the best and look good doing it.

» JOHNNY STOUT
Taking its cues from flora and fauna, the folder has movement, patterning, gold leaves and beastly handle scales. (*Eric Eggly, PointSeven image*)

« AARON WILBURN
In G-carta handle scales and an acorn shield, the back pocket slip-joint folder cuts the mustard via a CPM-154 stainless blade. (*BladeGallery.com image*)

BILL RUPLE
A tug on any of the three satin-finished CPM-154 blades will entice you to spend more time with the stag-handle sowbelly folder.
(BladeGallery.com image)

J.D. VAN DEVENTER
The front flipper folder models black and blue carbon fiber handle inlays and a satin-finished Sandvik 12C27 stainless blade.
(BladeGallery.com image)

K.C. GRAY
When red carbon fiber handle scales meet a Mike Norris "Fire Clone" damascus blade, the whole thing is just hot.
(SharpByCoop image)

STEVE HILL
The "Viral Vendetta" wards off global pandemics via a "wave" damascus blade, mottled green mammoth ivory handle scales, heat-colored damascus bolsters and a garnet set in the thumb stud.

JOHN DOYLE
Stylin' in a black G-10 handle and carbon fiber bolster, the "Topo Map" damascus flipper folder also showcases 24k-gold-plated screws and jeweled titanium liners. *(SharpByCoop image)*

⌵ A2—ANDRE VAN HEERDEN and ANDRE THORBURN
The South African makers combined a heat-colored Zladinox feather-pattern titanium damascus handle for the brilliant flipper folder with a Damasteel blade.

(BladeGallery.com image)

⌵ PHILIP BOOTH
The maker's "Minnow 18" scale-release auto comes in a CPM 154 blade and a Fat Carbon copper camo handle with copper inlays.

(Mitchell D. Cohen Photography)

» SCOTT GALLAGHER
The dress locking gent's folder is outfitted in "firecracker" damascus and mother-of-pearl.

(SharpByCoop image)

» EYAL LANDESMAN
The handle inlay on a "Siren" Damasteel dress locking folder is Eilat stone, which contains malachite, azurite, turquoise and other materials.

(SharpByCoop image)

» STEVE SKIFF
This custom "Culprit #52" flipper folder exhibits a CTS-XHP blade, a 3D milled titanium handle and a machined and anodized titanium bolster.

(BladeGallery.com image)

« MARIANO YANNONI
For his etched 52100 friction folder, the Argentinian knifemaker came up with a set of green G-10 handle scales to set on stainless liners.

(BladeGallery.com image)

⌄ FRANCOIS DU TOIT

A Timascus pivot collar accents the shredded carbon fiber handle of an RWL-34 stainless front flipper folder.

(BladeGallery.com image)

⌃ ANDRE VAN HEERDEN

A carbon fiber handle inlaid with ironwood is the pièce de résistance on a differentially finished CTS-XHP flipper folder. *(BladeGallery.com image)*

» CHRIS TAYLOR

The combination of vintage blue Westinghouse Ivorite and black-lip mother-of-pearl is strikingly handsome on the handle of a slip-joint folder with a Chad Nichols damascus blade.

(Cory Martin Imaging)

⌄ DAN DUGDALE

The handle of a D2 frame-lock folder is machined from .75-inch-diameter round titanium stock. *(SharpByCoop image)*

« KIRBY LAMBERT

Westinghouse paper Micarta handle scales give a W2 flipper folder a throwback look, even with the modern Mokuti pivot collars, titanium hardware and zirconium pocket clip. *(SharpByCoop image)*

« KOSIE STEENKAMP

A fantastic utility folder features a satin-finished Bohler N690 blade, antique Westinghouse Micarta handle and stacked carbon fiber and black G-10 bolsters.

(BladeGallery.com image)

❥ ANDRE THORBURN
An L48 front flipper showcases a san mai blade, silver twill handle scales set on anodized titanium liners, and zirconium bolsters inlaid with fine silver and engraved by Julien Marchal.
(BladeGallery.com image)

» PETER CAREY
Not all folders are created equal. The Scion model in a Chad Nichols Intrepid damascus blade and a meteorite-inlaid CarboQuartz handle with a custom zirconium pivot screw is one example. *(Mitchell D. Cohen Photography)*

« HERUCUS BLOMERUS
Captivatingly coordinated, the san mai flipper folder blends engraved and heat-colored zirconium bolsters with antique Westinghouse Micarta handle scales. *(BladeGallery. com image)*

⌃ PAUL KILBY
The carved and stippled titanium handle scales and bolsters really dress up the AEBL flipper folder.
(Eric Eggly, PointSeven image)

« ENRIQUE PENA
The South Texas Trapper looks dapper in a CPM-154 blade, stainless bolsters and a jigged bone handle.
(SharpByCoop image)

« SCOTT SAWBY
Black-lip mother-of-pearl inlays enliven the stainless steel frame of a "Woodcock" model Hitachi ATS-34 dress locking folder.
(SharpByCoop image)

» MICHAEL VAGNINO and KELLY VERMEER-VELLA
While Kelly forged a 1075-and-15N20 "Riptide" damascus blade and frame, Michael fashioned the dress locking folder, including black-lip-pearl handle inserts, timed damascus screws, a pearl-inlaid backbar and thumb stud and file-worked liners. *(SharpByCoop image)*

» BRIAN NADEAU
A trio of dress locking folders features NitroV and VegasForge stainless damascus blades and titanium, zirconium and AKS Timascus handles.

(SharpByCoop image)

« CRAIG BREWER
Housed within the confines of a five-blade stockman are CPM 154 blades and springs, integral 416 liners and bolsters, and stag covers. *(Caleb Royer image)*

» JOHN ARNOLD
Golden, copper and steel hues emit from the Damasteel folder with bronze and zirconium Mokumé bolsters forged by Chad Nichols and an antique Westinghouse Micarta grip.

(BladeGallery.com image)

« JAVIER VOGT
The guard-release auto is dressed in a high-carbon damascus blade, a stag handle, and zirconium bolsters.

(Eric Eggly, PointSeven image)

« JURGEN SCHANZ
A sculpted titanium handle dresses up a stainless damascus flipper folder forged from Sandvik 19C27 and 1.4034 steels.

(BladeGallery.com image)

» JEFF HALL
Copper shred carbon fiber gets a turn on a satin-finished "Viceroy" CPM-S35VN locking-liner folder with titanium liners.

(BladeGallery.com image)

« DAN THORNBURG
A winning combination of an elk antler handle, ADS Damascus bolsters, and a "Bifrost" Damasteel blade results in a "dressed for success folder."

(SharpByCoop image)

⌄ CRAIG BREWER
Choosing a select piece of stag was key for the slim folder with clip-point blade and long nail nick. *(Eric Eggly, PointSeven image)*

⌄ CHRIS SHARP
A "Lanny's Clip"-style slip-joint folder sports a CPM-154 blade, jigged bone handle scales, and an integral stainless bolster, liners and shield, the latter hollowed out in a patent-pending design.

(SharpByCoop image)

« TOBIN HILL
Natural stag and a Texas-shaped handle shield cover the stainless liners of a single-blade trapper in CPM-154 steel. *(Mitchell D. Cohen Photography)*

« CHARL PIENAAR
In a fit of inspiration, the maker decided to fashion the Bohler M390 stainless front flipper folder with a bead-blasted titanium frame and a jungle green Fat Carbon scale.

(BladeGallery.com image)

TREVOR BURGER
The Bohler M390 stainless locking-liner folder works off ceramic bearings and boasts a desert ironwood handle and carbon fiber bolsters.

(BladeGallery.com image)

JASON CLARK
The "Zulu" CTS-XHP locking-liner folder enlists a burlap Micarta handle, and burgundy linen Micarta bolsters, as well as an IKBS (Ikoma Korth Bearing System).

(BladeGallery.com image)

ERIC VANHESE
The "Mandalorian Field Blade," complete with bearing, spring and switch, looks sharp in a titanium handle and 15N20 blade.

(SharpByCoop image)

BILL and ERIC TUCH
A satin-finished "Sparrowhawk" dual-action, scale-release auto folder takes flight in titanium and CPM-S30V steel. *(Mitchell D. Cohen Photography)*

WILLEM STEENKAMP
It is a full-blown squall when "lightning strike" carbon fiber surrounds "Thunderstorm Kevlar" inlays for the handle of a CTS-XHP folder. *(BladeGallery.com image)*

TORY UTT
Ivory paper Micarta and G-10 make up the handle and bolster half of the damascus dress slip-joint folder with nickel silver liners, pins and shield. *(SharpByCoop image)*

» GEORGE MULLER
The combination of "Thor"-pattern Damasteel, Gibeon meteorite and Picasso marble is inspired and unmatched on most flipper folders.
(BladeGallery.com image)

⌃ RIAAN MANSER
If you are going to dress up a Bohler ELMAX flipper folder, you might as well use stabilized lacewood on titanium liners. *(BladeGallery.com image)*

⌄ DON HANSON III
After much admiration, close the damascus blade and thumb the walrus ivory grip as you slip the slip joint into a pants pocket.
(Caleb Royer image)

» CARL COLSON
A Damasteel dress locking folder gets a woolly mammoth tusk handle.
(SharpByCoop image)

⌃ BOB MERZ
A damascus interframe folder makes a nice entry with its wood handle inlay and file-worked spine. *(Eric Eggly, PointSeven image)*

« TYLER TURNER
Sometimes, a "Bulldog" slip-joint folder just needs a little European red stag to spruce it up.
(Mitchell D. Cohen Photography)

» DALE MILLER
Gent's folders deserve damascus blades, "explosion"-pattern bolsters, and flush-end mammoth ivory handle scales.
(BladeGallery.com image)

⌄ TIM ROBERTSON
Few will ever tire of deeply grooved, natural stag-handle folders, nor should they. *(Eric Eggly, PointSeven image)*

» SEAN O'HARE
The smooth Mini Rambler flipper steps out in a satin-finished CTS-XHP stainless blade, a stabilized curly Koa handle, and marbled carbon-fiber bolsters.
(BladeGallery.com image)

« R.J. MARTIN
Sometimes, it takes a grooved and groovy "Dragon Fire Timascus" handle, and zirconium bolsters to dress up an S110V tactical folder.
(SharpByCoop image)

» RICHARD S. WRIGHT
Of the ambidextrous bolster-release switchblade ilk, there is nothing standard about the ladder-pattern damascus blade and bolsters, carved back bar in a dragon and leaf motif or the coffee-colored mammoth ivory handle scales.
(SharpByCoop image)

« JEFF VANDERMEULEN
There's so much character inherent within the "Grosserosen" Damasteel blade and "Boomerang" Zircuti handle of the dress locking folder.
(SharpByCoop image)

Interesting Tactics

There is something a little straighter, more in line and true about a tactical knife fashioned for the military or martial arts. Like a stiff-backed soldier, the knives wear their uniforms with pride, stand at the ready and await their commands.

Not only is there a look to a true tactical knife, but a feel, as if the pointed blade projects its purpose upon the rest of the piece. The features are not fashioned for aesthetics or frills but balance, palpability, protection and power.

Edges are not blunted, big-bellied or boxy, but keen and true. Guards are just large enough to keep hands and fingers from edges, and handles are meant to be cradled, gripped, squeezed and enveloped. Every inch of an interesting tactic is planned and purpose-built.

Their users rely on them, stand by the edges and salute the makers. The tactics are as interesting as the operators, and the two belong together.

⩖ **ALEX HOSSOM**
The "Karambitch" is all attitude, including a CPM-3V blade, ivory Micarta grip and mosaic pins. *(Mitchell D. Cohen Photography)*

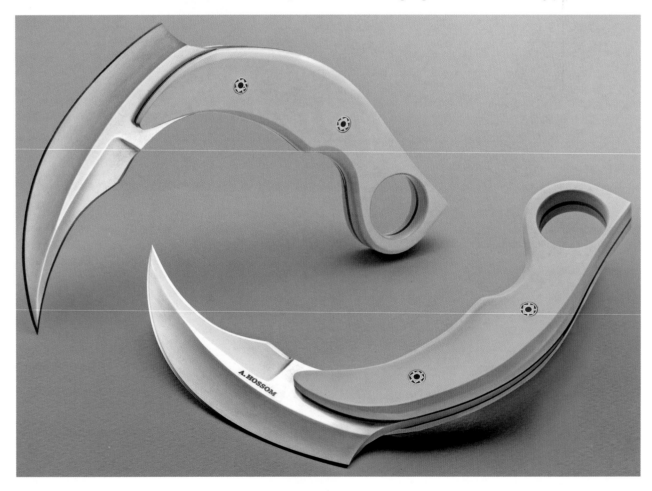

《 LEE LERMAN
The entire CDP D2
"Hydra" frame-lock
flipper folder is wet glass
blasted, including the
zirconium handle scales
and titanium bolsters,
liners and pocket clip.
(Mitchell D. Cohen Photography)

》 JONATHAN MCNEES
A "Sodbuster Front
Flipper" is designed
with a CPM-20CV blade,
titanium handle and
black Timascus pocket
clip. *(SharpByCoop image)*

》 KOSIE STEENKAMP
A Thunderstorm Kevlar
bolster has tactical
written all over it, as
does the green Micarta
handle of a Bohler
N690 stainless flipper.
(BladeGallery.com image)

**《 PETER and CORY
MARTIN**
Butterscotch Micarta
is sticky sweet on a
double-guarded, folding,
stonewashed 12C27
stainless dagger. *(Cory
Martin Imaging)*

» K.C. GRAY
With a name like "Hellbender Dagger," expectations run high for the titanium-frame Sm100 folder with zirconium thumb disc. *(SharpByCoop image)*

« RIAAN MANSER
A Bohler ELMAX stainless flipper folder parades a black G-10 handle with bird's-eye maple inlays. *(BladeGallery.com image)*

» MATT GREGORY and SAM TAYLOR
Weighing in at only 5 ounces, the tanto sports a Russian BT23 Armor titanium blade, a Richlite guard and a wrapped Terotuf and carbon fiber handle. *(SharpByCoop image)*

⌃ JEREMY MARSH
Making its point clear, the "Zirc Chisel" folder embodies a CPM-154 blade, zirconium handle scales, titanium liners and 3-D zirconium thumb studs. *(Mitchell D. Cohen Photography)*

≪ J.D. VAN DEVENTER
A no-frills tactical flipper folder exhibits a Bohler N690 blade working off an IKBS (Ikoma Korth Bearing System), zirconium bolsters and carbon fiber handle scales. *(BladeGallery.com image)*

≪ ROBERT APPLEBY
A Tom Maringer styled "Haiku" fighter is defined by an upswept AEB-L blade and a wire-wrapped bamboo handle. *(SharpByCoop image)*

≪ PAT BIGGIN
Designed for a martial arts instructor as a gift from his students, the black and red paper Micarta handle represents the black belt ranking that the teacher holds. *(Cory Martin Imaging)*

≪ TASHI BHARUCHA
A titanium frame-lock flipper folder is presented in a mean and clean CPM-154 blade.
(Mitchell D. Cohen Photography)

» JON MOORE
It does not get much more "tactical" than a blade forged from the timing chain of a Humvee returning from Iraq married with a stacked leather washer handle.

⌃» RAIMUND LHOTAK
The tactical combo has heat-treated ATI425 titanium blades, and OD green canvas Micarta handles with red G-10 liners. *(SharpByCoop image)*

« JERRY HOSSOM
One "Flyover" is all you need, this one in a 5.5-inch CTS-XHP blade, black canvas Micarta handle and red liners.
(Mitchell D. Cohen Photography)

Fine Cuts of Cloth

Old rag Micarta doesn't sound very appealing, does it? One does not often hear about "old pearl," "past-its-prime curly maple," "dated damascus" or "senior abalone" handle slabs. Yet, like movies, wine, cheeses, books and even people, some age well and others do not.

Old rag Micarta ages to perfection. Knifemakers seek old rag and Westinghouse Micarta out for its classic colors, character and condition.

Canvas Micarta does not crack or break and rarely needs cleaning or repair. It feels good in the hand, has a throwback look and makes knives appear mean and lean at the same time.

Not everything ages well, but fine cuts of cloth do—particularly rag and canvas Micarta applied cleanly onto knives in the form of handle scales.

⌄ **BILL RUPLE**
The "Bow Trapper" sports a CPM-154 blade, 416 stainless liners and hardware, old rag Micarta handle scales and red liners. *(Mitchell D. Cohen Photography)*

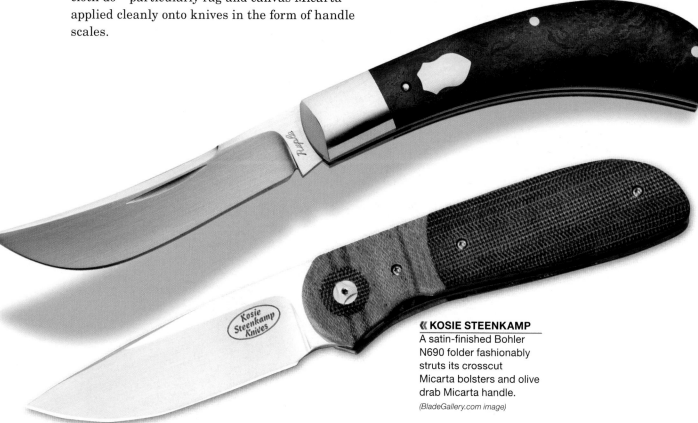

《 **KOSIE STEENKAMP**
A satin-finished Bohler N690 folder fashionably struts its crosscut Micarta bolsters and olive drab Micarta handle.
(BladeGallery.com image)

KYLE HANSON
Vintage canvas Micarta adds even more character to an already intriguing hunter in a W2 blade with a smoky temper line. Kenny Rowe fashioned the sheath for the piece. *(SharpByCoop image)*

PETER CAREY
The CPM 154 flipper folders with green canvas Micarta handle scales and titanium liners and frames arrived in pairs. *(Mitchell D. Cohen Photography)*

K.C. GRAY
A hawksbill CPM-154 tactical folder has satin-finished, bead-blasted titanium bolsters and green canvas Micarta handle scales. *(SharpByCoop image)*

DENIS BUDAK
The full-dress folder includes a san mai blade, textured titanium bolsters, a vintage military rag Micarta handle and mammoth ivory inlays. *(Caleb Royer image)*

JASON CLARK
Canvas Micarta is dovetailed into burgundy Micarta for the handle and bolsters of the Zulu front flipper folder featuring a Damasteel blade. *(BladeGallery.com image)*

⌄ JEFF HALL
One "Bounty Hunter" damascus folding tanto arrives at the scene in zirconium bolsters, and green canvas Micarta handle scales

(BladeGallery.com image)

» DAN BIDINGER
A contoured burlap and green canvas Micarta handle, with carbon fiber spacer, anchors the satin-finished A2 chef's knife. *(BladeGallery.com image)*

» DON HANSON III
Rag Micarta handle scales suffice for the "Shadow" slip joint in a W2 blade.

(Caleb Royer image)

» WILLEM STEENKAMP
Green canvas Micarta and carbon fiber give the CTS-XHP flipper folder a throwback look and feel.

(BladeGallery.com image)

⌃ MAVERICK MURDOCK
The combination of canvas Micarta handle scales, antiqued bronze bolsters, and a sculpted 1084 blade is impressive. *(SharpByCoop image)*

Born in the U.S.A.
Bowies

» ANDREW BURKE
Damascus and stag bowies are a staple in the industry, this piece featuring a twist pattern and a 416 stainless bolster.
(BladeGallery.com image)

» JOHN DOYLE
The bowie enters the fray wearing a W2 blade, bronze guard and collar, and an African blackwood handle with curly maple inlays.
(SharpByCoop image)

« JEREMY BARTLETT
Do the twist-damascus bowie and rattle that curly Koa handle.
(Caleb Royer image)

« DAVID LISCH
Equal parts awesome are the feather damascus and sambar stag of a vest pocket bowie.
(SharpByCoop image)

» ANDERS HOGSTROM
The aptly named "Blue Bird" rancher bowie blends a 1050 blade with a blue/brown fossil walrus ivory handle. The fittings are carved, textured and antiqued sterling silver.
(Mitchell D. Cohen Photography)

⌄ BEN AKIN
Of the camp bowie type, the W2 carbon steel blade has been clay-zone heat treated and combined with an antique wrought iron guard and a Bocote handle. *(BladeGallery.com image)*

» SCOTT GALLAGHER
With one winsome damascus blade, the take-down bowie has a blacked-out damascus guard and a mahogany dyed stag grip.
(SharpByCoop image)

» KELLY FRASIER and JON KELLY
Honduran mahogany appears on a 1075 high-carbon ring guard bowie with a copper guard.
(SharpByCoop image)

MIKE CLARK
More of a drop-point than clip-point gent's bowie, the satin-finished san mai blade is held at bay by a premium sambar stag handle and blued mild steel guard.
(BladeGallery.com image)

JIM COFFEE
The classic bowie is built correctly in a 220-layer random-pattern damascus blade, hot-blued fittings and a sambar stag grip.
(Caleb Royer image)

CURTIS HAALAND
Put in my order for a "Generations Bowie" in a W1 tool steel blade, mild steel guard and stabilized Koa handle, please.
(SharpByCoop image)

BRUNO DAL MOLIN
A bowie was born from some cracked ivory and a billet of tightly patterned damascus steel. *(Caleb Royer image)*

⏫ BLAKE NICHOLS
It's not like you can go to the hardware store and pick up a differentially heat-treated 1075 bowie with a wrought iron guard and Tasmanian blackwood handle. *(SharpByCoop image)*

⏫ TAD LYNCH
The wavy temper line of the master smith's W2 blade adds movement to the bowie, properly handled in walrus ivory.

(SharpByCoop image)

⏫ ERIK MCCRIGHT
Building big bowies in tightly patterned damascus and burl is never a bad thing.

(Eric Eggly, PointSeven image)

⏫ ANDERS HOGSTROM
The "Border Town Bowie" hits the streets in a 1050 clip-point blade, antiqued sterling silver guard and an ancient walrus ivory handle. *(BladeGallery.com image)*

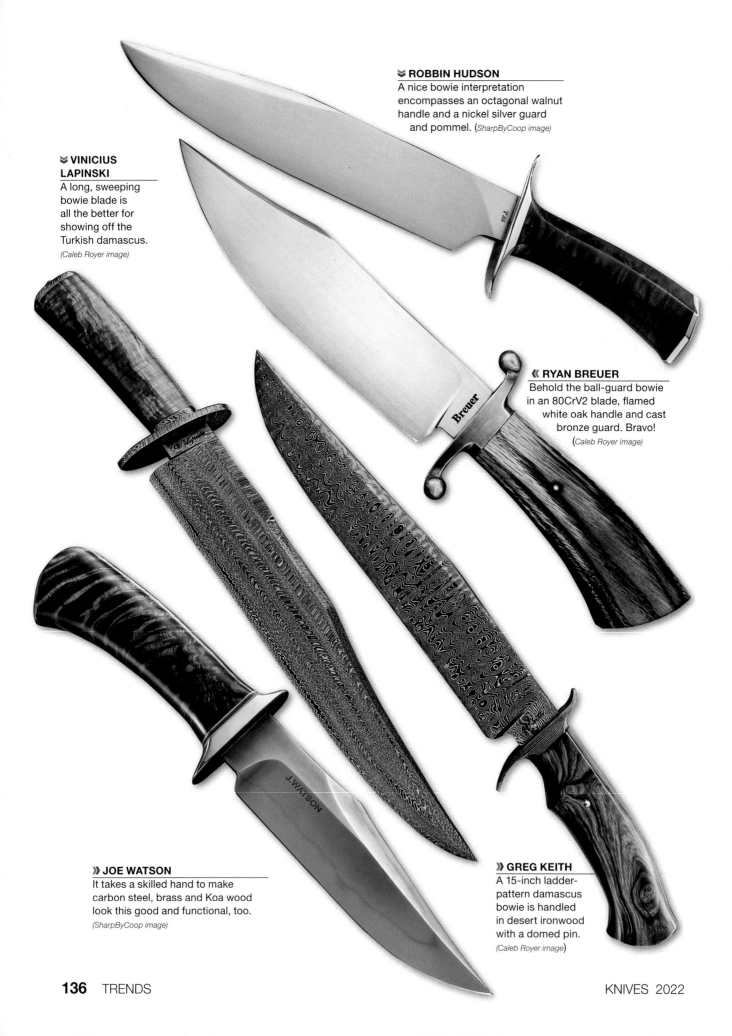

ROBBIN HUDSON
A nice bowie interpretation encompasses an octagonal walnut handle and a nickel silver guard and pommel. *(SharpByCoop image)*

VINICIUS LAPINSKI
A long, sweeping bowie blade is all the better for showing off the Turkish damascus.

(Caleb Royer image)

RYAN BREUER
Behold the ball-guard bowie in an 80CrV2 blade, flamed white oak handle and cast bronze guard. Bravo!
(Caleb Royer image)

JOE WATSON
It takes a skilled hand to make carbon steel, brass and Koa wood look this good and functional, too.

(SharpByCoop image)

GREG KEITH
A 15-inch ladder-pattern damascus bowie is handled in desert ironwood with a domed pin.
(Caleb Royer image)

» JOSH WISOR
Let loose the Turkish twist damascus bowie and behold its fossil mammoth ivory grip.
(SharpByCoop image)

⌄ BARRY CLODFELTER
The way he builds them, the fans will keep coming, with this bowie in a 540-layer twist-damascus blade, stainless guard and Tasmanian blackwood grip.
(Caleb Royer image)

⌃ MARK KNAPP
Cholla cactus, desert ironwood and turquoise are combined for the handle of a "High Desert Bowie" in a 1095 blade.
(SharpByCoop image)

» JIM PROVOST
Taking one's eyes off the stabilized splayed beech handle long enough to admire the rest of the CPM-154 hidden-tang bowie knife is not so easy.
(SharpByCoop image)

« TED THORNTON
For a classic bowie, the maker planished the stainless guard and butt cap, adding a 440C blade, and an African blackwood and vulcanized paper handle. *(Caleb Royer image)*

» JORDON BERTHELOT
The re-curved bowie benefits from a Justin Reynolds tri-stack damascus blade, brass guard and pommel, and a sika stag handle from The Stag Depot.
(Caleb Royer image)

« ALEXANDER NOOT
The "Hos Megas" bowie is a seven-bar Turkish twist damascus behemoth with an O1 edge, a forge-welded damascus guard and an amber stag handle.
(Caleb Royer image)

» JOSH SMITH
This little bowie that could is dressed in stag, damascus and a nicely sculpted guard for good measure. *(Eric Eggly, PointSeven image)*

« JAMES WHITE
A forged 5160 bowie is outfitted in a giraffe bone handle, Mokume and brass spacers, and a Kenny Rowe carved leather sheath.
(SharpByCoop image)

» MATT ROBERTS
A Southeast bowie blends a forged 1075 blade with a stainless guard and a faux Westinghouse paper Micarta handle.
(SharpByCoop image)

PAUL COOPER
Born in the U.S.A. is an etched 1095 "Liberty Justice" bowie with an elk horn handle and wrought iron guard. *(SharpByCoop image)*

BILL BURKE
Incorporating a 10-inch, hand-forged, differentially heat treated 5160 blade, the bowie is secured by a 416 stainless guard and sambar stag grip. *(BladeGallery.com image)*

AIDAN GARRITY
A shapely green linen Micarta handle and 440C stainless guard lend credence to the "Legitimus" name of the 1095 bowie.
(SharpByCoop image)

JIM POOR
A Turkish twist bowie is built with a mammoth ivory handle and a clamshell-style 1075 high carbon steel guard. *(SharpByCoop image)*

KELLY VERMEER-VELLA
Of takedown construction with a damascus screw, the bowie is built from damascus, mild steel, titanium and mammoth ivory. *(SharpByCoop image)*

» JACKSON RUMBLE
Stag-handle bowies
might be a staple, but
they do not get any
sweeter than the satin-
finished 1084 model here.

(BladeGallery.com image)

« LUKE HAAG
Built during Kyle Royer's
online knifemaking course, the
take-down bowie is designed
with a 5160 blade, wrought
iron fittings and a stabilized
Tasmanian blackwood handle.

(Caleb Royer image)

« DAVE LARSEN
If you're out for
"Retribution," the
aptly named O1 bowie
with Koa handle and
plum-brown mild
steel guard, spacer
and pommel might
not be a bad choice.

(SharpByCoop image)

**⌃ CODY HOFSOMMER
and PEYTON RAMM**
 A collaboration by
Season 7 "Forged in Fire"
champions, the bowie
boasts a damascus blade
and mammoth ivory handle.

(SharpByCoop image)

⌃ NICK BACHTEL
Occasionally, you
feel like forging
a 9-inch 80CrV2
camp bowie with
an elk tine handle,
blued steel furniture
and brass accents.

(Caleb Royer image)

JAMES FLEMING
In an ode to the fossilized mammoth ivory handle, the aptly named "Permafrost Bowie" sports a mosaic damascus blade and a 14k-gold-brazed guard, frame, liners and spacer.
(SharpByCoop image)

DAVID DAVIS
The hidden-tang bowie sports a sambar stag handle, 5160 steel blade, stainless guard, and bone, nickel silver and black-fiber spacers.
(Caleb Royer image)

ARTUR SZYNGWELSKI
The big bowie boasts a Patryk Pawlik damascus blade and leather sheath, a carbon fiber guard and a white G-10 handle. *(Caleb Royer image)*

PEYTON RAMM
A penny-guard bowie parades a 1084-and-15N20 damascus blade, mammoth ivory handle scales, engraving and gold inlay. *(SharpByCoop image)*

ADAM MILLE
This one had 'em hook, line and sinker, particularly the canister damascus blade of nickel fishing hooks forged together with 1080 and 1095 high carbon steels, as well as the fossilized walrus ivory handle.
(SharpByCoop image)

Built for the
Boot Knives

There is something about not only carrying a knife but wearing it that makes toting a blade more of an intimate experience. Whether in a cross-draw sheath, with a neck bead chain, on the hip or in the boot, wearing a knife on the person, and not just in the pocket, gives one a sense of security and purpose.

Boot knives are akin to pocket pistols or vest-pocket bowies, and have been around since police have been undercover, gamblers and conmen have been in operation, and special forces have gone covert and stealth.

Reaching into the boot is not as much of a stretch as one might think, and sometimes it is good to get down onto one knee to assess a situation anyway. So, why not carry a knife built for the boot? We can always use another blade on our person, in case we lose one, of course.

» NATHAN CAROTHERS
The blade of a hollow-ground CPM-3V boot dagger becomes more of a flat grind toward the tip, where it twists slightly to reinforce the point, all anchored by a checkered black Micarta handle and outfitted with a Jill Gregory sheath. *(SharpByCoop image)*

» STEVE AUVENSHINE
A Texas boot knife is done up nicely in a 1095 blade, mesquite wood handle and sterling silver guard.

(SharpByCoop image)

« MAMORU SHIGENO
Check out the fuller on the "special boot knife," as well as the sharp lines of the ATS-34 blade, the blackened zirconium fittings and the Timascus handle and screws.

(SharpByCoop image)

» ANDERS HOGSTROM
Straight and true is the boot dagger in a 1050 carbon steel blade, sculpted copper guard and beech burl handle.

(SharpByCoop image)

Multi-Blade Parade

« CRAIG BREWER
A lock-back whittler gets the full treatment—CPM-154 blades and springs, and some of the sweetest mammoth ivory this side of the Alaskan frontier.

(SharpByCoop image)

⌃ TOM PLOPPERT
Single-, three- and five-blade "Diamond Edge Cattle Knives" feature CPM-154 steel, 416 stainless bolsters and ebony handle scales. *(SharpByCoop image)*

⌃ TIM ROBERTSON
A saddlehorn pattern is appropriately executed in ancient ivory and steel.

(Eric Eggly, PointSeven image)

⌃ LUKE SWENSON
No ordinary trapper, the comely model uses CPM-154 blade steel, 416 stainless bolsters and jeweled stainless liners.
(Mitchell D. Cohen Photography)

》TOBIN HILL
The CPM-154 steel legs are long on a double lock-back trapper, and the amber stag body slim and sloping.
(SharpByCoop image)

》ROAN WEST
The maker shows where he's from on the handle and what he's got with the double rope file work along the blade spines.
(SharpByCoop image)

⌃ RICK DUNKERLEY
Scroll engraving, file-worked liners and damascus steel are classy touches reserved for a two-blade pocketknife.
(Eric Eggly, PointSeven image)

BILL RUPLE
Of the three-blade split-back canoe whittler ilk, the folder is fashioned using CPM 154 and stainless steels, as well as mammoth ivory handle scales.
(Mitchell D. Cohen Photography)

BILL KENNEDY JR.
In a muskrat style, the folder comes alive in dense-twist Damasteel blades, Alaskan mammoth ivory handle scales and engraving by Paul Markow.
(SharpByCoop image)

STANLEY BUZEK
At 3.75 inches closed, the CPM 154 stainless folder sports long-pull clip and beavertail spay blades, fluted bolsters, mammoth ivory handle scales and a bollock shield. *(Eric Eggly, PointSeven image)*

CHRIS SHARP
The more blades, the better, when you can build them like the etched 15N20-and-1075 damascus edges of the trapper featuring bark mammoth ivory handle scales and integral bolsters, liners and shield. *(SharpByCoop image)*

Full-Blown
Integrals

The ones who build the integrals, with blades, guards, tangs, and often pommels being one solid piece of steel, are the group's hotrodders. Yeah, they pull those engines from the muscle cars, replace any part that is not solid and working perfectly, polish the steel, chrome out the parts and possibly bore out the engines for more torque and horsepower. They change their own oil, by the way.

And like the cars, these are solid knives, or they better be—they are steel and handle slabs. They have edges, they work, and they are powerful but not easy to make.

It takes a little planning and a lot of wrangling to build 'em out of one piece of steel, tried and true, straight and honed to a keen edge. There is little room for error, like a big block engine coming out of a Pontiac 389—there's not much wiggle room.

They like to go full-bore, with full-blown integrals, designed to cut, built to last.

» SAMUEL LURQUIN
A matched set made for a father and daughter, the Tsavo integral sub-hilt fighter and small integral sport damascus blades and bolsters, ironwood handles and shark skin-inlaid leather sheaths by Jeremy Guillaume.
(SharpByCoop image)

KEVIN HARVEY
A full-integral Gyuto chef's knife is dressed in damascus from head to foot or tip to butt.

(BladeGallery.com image)

» JASON ELLARD
The mosaic damascus is so gorgeous, it needed to be made into an integral, from the blade and bolster straight through to pommel, with fiddleback Tasmanian blackwood covering the tang of the chef's knife.

(SharpByCoop image)

« BLAINE STEPHENSON
The canister-steel 52100- and-1095 damascus integral fixed blade is outfitted with mammoth ivory handle scales.

(Caleb Royer image)

《 CARL COLSON
With an integral CPM-154 blade, frame and bolsters, Rocky Mountain bighorn handle scales lend warmth to the steely drop-point hunter.
(SharpByCoop image)

》 BILL BEHNKE
Of curly Koa and 1085 steel, the full-tang integral is nicely put together. *(Eric Eggly, PointSeven image)*

》 MARCUS LIN
A Bob Loveless design, the Hip Pocket Hunter is of one-piece, integral construction with a drop-point RWL-34 blade and a Westinghouse rag Micarta handle.
(Caleb Royer image)

⌃ JJ. ALEX RUIZ
The forged, full-tang integral is accomplished in 5160 steel and an Elforyn Super Tusk (faux elephant ivory) handle.
(Caleb Royer image)

» MIKE QUESENBERRY
The forged-to-shape 52100 integral hunter wears its fossil walrus ivory scales with pride, not to mention the 18k-gold pins.
(Caleb Royer image)

⌃ RALEIGH AVERY
Forged from an antique heirloom railroad spike, the handle of the integral piece is Indian mahogany.
(Caleb Royer image)

⌃ JAYDEN SIMISKY
A 5160 integral keyhole fixed blade is treated to a sub-critical anneal and given a box elder burl handle. *(Caleb Royer image)*

« AARON SYBRANT
Forging the 52100 integral camp knife and sanding it by hand, the maker chose a sweet slab of amboyna burl for the grip.
(SharpByCoop image)

Striking Fighters

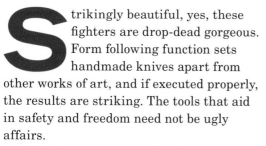

Strikingly beautiful, yes, these fighters are drop-dead gorgeous. Form following function sets handmade knives apart from other works of art, and if executed properly, the results are striking. The tools that aid in safety and freedom need not be ugly affairs.

With their straight backs, slim profiles and pointed tips, the soldiers fight on, guarded, focused, deadly. They are also workhorses, cutting with aplomb and severing with ease, nary a tear in the media through which they slice.

Handles are meant to be gripped, blades for thrusting and slashing, and points to puncture.

Like trained, muscled prizefighters, they do more than jab and counter-punch. They are utilitarian beasts best kept sheathed until needed. That is the nature of the beast. It does not lash out unless provoked and can be a striking being, toned, true, bold and beautiful.

» GREG KEITH
A curved fuller gives a ladder-pattern damascus fighter with desert ironwood handle further flow.
(Caleb Royer image)

» ETHAN LEE
A fixed fighter like Daryl Dixon's knife in the TV show "The Walking Dead," the pretty piece parades a 10-inch damascus blade with a sawtooth spine, an antiqued brass guard and frame, and Gabon ebony handle.
(SharpByCoop image)

⌄ JOHN DINGMAN

There are few straight lines on the 440C stainless steel sub-hilt fighter in a bloodwood handle, and that is a good thing. *(Eric Eggly, PointSeven image)*

⌄ BOB EARHART

Twist damascus, purple heartwood and blued stainless steel make up the bulk of the F-35 Fighter, named after the F-35 Lightning II fighter jet due to its sleek design and aggressive looks. *(SharpByCoop image)*

⌄ DAVID MCCONNELL

Dyed and stabilized curly mango just sounds sweet and looks the part on a 1075 fighter with gun-blued mild steel guard. *(Cory Martin Imaging)*

⌃ JOSH WISOR

The maker's Persian-inspired dagger is delivered in a mosaic damascus blade, antiqued brass guard and carved ringed Gidgee handle. *(SharpByCoop image)*

⌃ KELLY VERMEER-VELLA

The fighter squadron stands ready in a 1075-and-15N20 damascus blade, mild steel guard and fossil ivory handle. *(SharpByCoop image)*

MARK BANFIELD
A wicked recurved fighter comes in a hand-forged 1075 blade, a heat-blued wrought iron guard and a carved ancient bog oak handle.
(BladeGallery.com image)

ALEX HOSSOM
A stunningly beautiful "Kopis" model parades a 12-inch damascus blade and a California buckeye burl handle.
(Mitchell D. Cohen Photography)

DAVID BROADWELL and STEVE RANDALL
While Steve forged the laminated steel blade, David got busy carving out a mammoth ivory handle and sculpting a damascus guard and bronze trim.
(SharpByCoop image)

JEFF DAVIDSON
The full-tang, wood-handle fighter with carbon fiber bolsters, red, black and copper liners and mosaic pins has a lot of reach and appeal. *(Eric Eggly, PointSeven image)*

AIDAN GARRITY
Stabilized oak burl plays a starring role on the 1095 "Galloglas Bowie."
(SharpByCoop image)

JOE WATSON
The forged carbon steel blade shows off a rolling hamon (temper line) and sharpened clip, while the handle is carved and stabilized Hawaiian Koa wood. Paul Long fashioned a sheath for the piece. *(Caleb Royer image)*

DERICK KEMPER
The "Twisted" integral fighter is done up in a W2 blade and a Thuya burl handle. *(SharpByCoop image)*

JON MOORE
A high-carbon steel fighter, the blade has been acid etched, and the curly maple handle dyed red.

MARCUS LIN
A Bob Loveless "Dixon Fighter," made from the original pattern in the Loveless shop, sports an RWL-34 blade, a stainless guard and a black canvas Micarta handle. *(SharpByCoop image)*

LUKAS SCHOENBORN
From its pointed pommel to the tip of the damascus blade, the fighter is a fierce contender. *(Eric Eggly, PointSeven image)*

⌃ ANDERS HOGSTROM
There's a lot of fight in the 11.5-inch recurved 1050 blade of the "Hyena," complete with an ironwood handle and textured and antiqued bronze fittings. *(Mitchell D. Cohen Photography)*

⌃ JIM WHITE
Grab ahold of that exhibition grade Koa handle on the 5150 fighter, and don't let go.

(SharpByCoop image)

⌃ DEON NEL
The Bob Loveless-style battle knife enlists a hollow-ground, mirror-polished N690 blade and a maroon Micarta handle. *(BladeGallery.com image)*

⌃ MATTHEW GREGORY
A cord-wrapped amboyna burl handle and CPM-S45Vn blade make up the better part of a Kwaiken fixed fighter.

(SharpByCoop image)

⌃ CHARLES CARPENTER
A clip-point fighter is fashioned with a Texas Wind pattern damascus blade, copper spacers and a curly Hawaiian koa handle.

(Caleb Royer image)

GARY MARTINDALE
The finely fit-and-finished sub-hilt fighter features a CPM-154 blade, amber jigged bone handle, red liners and stainless guard.
(SharpByCoop image)

BILL POOR
It is a lot to take in—the length of recurved damascus blade, thumb notches, finger guard and canvas Micarta handle.
(Eric Eggly, PointSeven image)

STUART SMITH
The prettiest fighter on the block struts its "W's"-pattern damascus blade and C-guard, hand-fluted ironwood handle and bronze fittings.
(BladeGallery.com image)

ALAN MITCHELL
The "Half Moon Fighter" welcomes twilight in a damascus blade, sandblasted and hot-blued mild steel guard, and an African blackwood grip.

JIM HAMMOND
A 30th-anniversary spin-off design, the fixed fighter is executed in a slotted BG-42 blade, and Scottish red stag handle scales.
(SharpByCoop image)

Ringing
Historically True

Whether history is oral or written, photographed or charted, recorded or lived, it can be referenced and appreciated. Those steeped in history have an informed perspective of the present and understand what it took to get here.

Historically accurate knives are also culturally significant. For most edged tools and weapons, form follows function, and function has traditionally been a product of environmental, social and communal forces. The knives people use are dictated by how and where the community lives—its basic needs, activities and chores.

Once the forms of knives are determined, embellishments are added, and the people's tastes start to shine through, a cultural identity in cut. The knives and swords on this and the following pages speak of the people who came before, whether they lived in the African, Asian, European or American continents, and in the last century or eons ago. They ring historically true, and we could all use a little more of that in the modern world.

« MATT GREGORY and RICK MARCHAND
Going by the name "Quarantanto," the rough-forged L-6 Japanese beauty exhibits a Terotuf frame, Richilite and copper tsuba (guard) and a cord-wrapped handle covered in dark brown Tsukaito and soaked in resin.
(SharpByCoop image)

☆ **ALAN MITCHEL**

The unusual angle of the red bushwillow handle on a French kitchen knife makes it easy to slice food without the chef's hand stopping the downward action of the damascus blade.

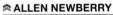

☆ **JERRY VAN EIZENGA**

The wide double-edged, tapered blade, round, stacked spacer handle, ball guard, and pronounced pommel are indicative of World War II theater knives. *(Eric Eggly, PointSeven image)*

☆ **ALLEN NEWBERRY**

Dinner will reach the table in record speed using the clay hardened W2 blade of the Santoku, but hold onto that African blackwood handle.

(Caleb Royer image)

☆ **ANDERS HOGSTROM**

Pass the Persian fighter in Damasteel, sterling silver, bronze and fossil walrus ivory, please. *(SharpByCoop image)*

« FOREST "BUTCH" SHEELY
A historically authentic pipe tomahawk showcases a mild steel and 52100 head, a curly maple handle and nickel silver insets. *(Eric Eggly, PointSeven image)*

» MAURICIO DALETZKY
A South American gaucho knife features a forged-to-shape Spirograph damascus blade and a crosscut "zebra waves" carbon fiber handle.
(BladeGallery.com image)

» JORDON BERTHELOT
The maker's take on a Nessmuk knife used and popularized by George Washington Sears involves an Elmax blade and a dogwood handle from Scott Johns Scale Workz.
(Caleb Royer image)

« MACE VITALE
Indonesian in origin, the "Tail of the Tiger" kris waves its damascus blade like it is the island country's flag.
(SharpByCoop image)

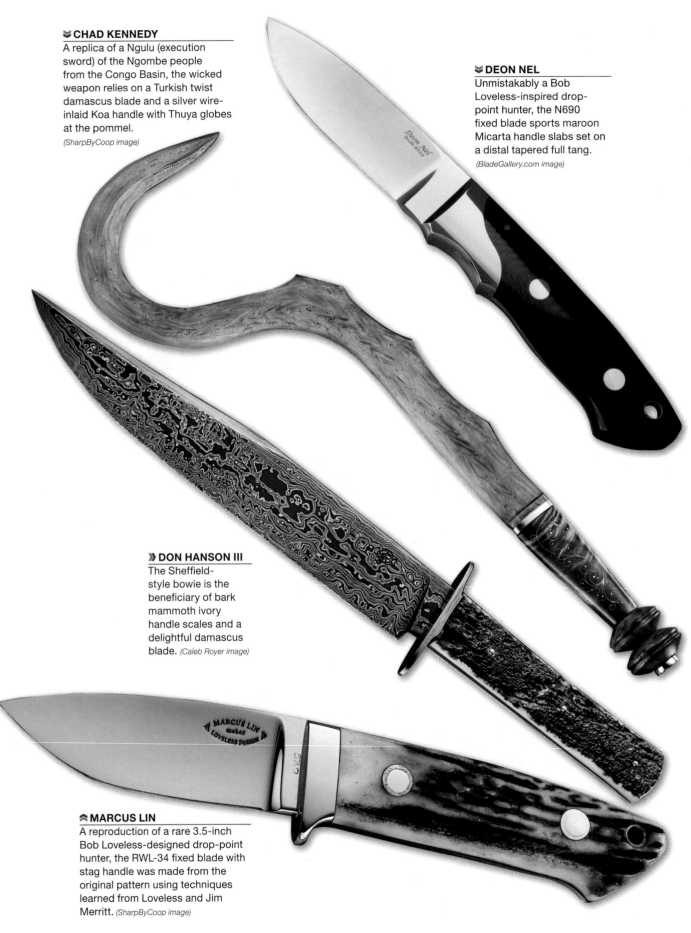

⌄ CHAD KENNEDY
A replica of a Ngulu (execution sword) of the Ngombe people from the Congo Basin, the wicked weapon relies on a Turkish twist damascus blade and a silver wire-inlaid Koa handle with Thuya globes at the pommel.

(SharpByCoop image)

⌄ DEON NEL
Unmistakably a Bob Loveless-inspired drop-point hunter, the N690 fixed blade sports maroon Micarta handle slabs set on a distal tapered full tang.

(BladeGallery.com image)

» DON HANSON III
The Sheffield-style bowie is the beneficiary of bark mammoth ivory handle scales and a delightful damascus blade. *(Caleb Royer image)*

⌃ MARCUS LIN
A reproduction of a rare 3.5-inch Bob Loveless-designed drop-point hunter, the RWL-34 fixed blade with stag handle was made from the original pattern using techniques learned from Loveless and Jim Merritt. *(SharpByCoop image)*

《 RICHARD S. WRIGHT
Based on an antique Spanish folding knife, the ambidextrous bolster-release switchblade sports a random pattern damascus blade, checkered ivory handle scales and a carved titanium back bar and liners.

》 JOSH RIDER
The maker's take on a Kwaiken fighter involves a 26c3 blade with pronounced hamon (temper line) and a cord-wrapped forged carbon fiber handle. *(SharpByCoop image)*

》 WILLIAM KALKBRENNER
The maker whipped up a Honyaki Gyuto chef's knife featuring a hand-forged W2 carbon steel blade with a Japanese clay zone hamon, an antiqued copper bolster and Gabon ebony handle.

(BladeGallery.com image)

⌃ KEVIN HARVEY
The white pearwood and bone handle of a "W's"-pattern damascus Nordic hunter look much like the traditional birch often used. *(BladeGallery.com image)*

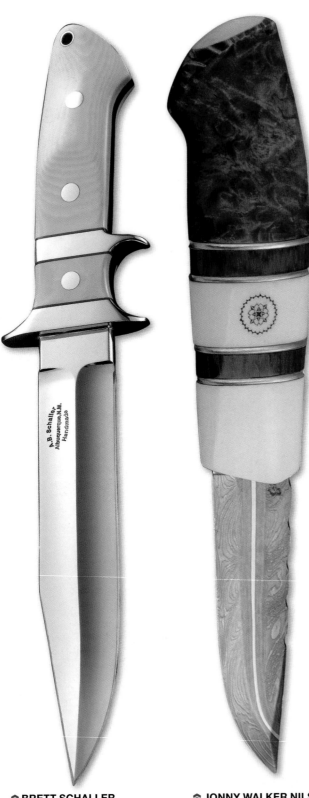

⌃ **BRETT SCHALLER**
Like Bob Loveless himself would have built it, the sub-hilt fighter sports a CPM-154 blade, an antique ivory Micarta handle and red liners and spacers.

(SharpByCoop image)

⌃ **JONNY WALKER NILSSON**
A traditionally styled puukko parades a Mattias Styrefors multi-bar composite damascus blade, a masur birch, snakewood and engraved reindeer antler handle and pewter spacers.

(BladeGallery.com image)

⌃ **PABLO DANIEL QUAGLINO**
A Spanish belduque is orchestrated in random pattern damascus, Guayacan wood and copper pins.

(SharpByCoop image)

⌃ **MATT GASKILL**
The forged integral Gurkha kukri is 1095 steel with a smoky hamon, a desert ironwood handle and brass pins.

(Caleb Royer image)

⌄ SHANE TAYLOR

The maker's version of a Gurkha kukri relies on a damascus blade, forged bronze guard in a skull motif and a cocobolo handle.

(BladeGallery.com image)

« CRAIG CAMERER

Of the Nessmuk hunter variety, the 1,800-layer damascus blade is accompanied by a stag handle and a lightweight but sturdy carbon fiber guard and spacers.

(Caleb Royer image)

« KEN HALL

The twist damascus Scottish sgian dubh enlists an African blackwood handle and a giraffe bone pommel stone.

(SharpByCoop image)

⌃ MARDI MESHEJIAN

The carved handle and san mai damascus blade of the sgian dubh, as well as the wooden sheath, are strikingly beautiful.

(SharpByCoop image)

» JARROD FISCUS
With pewter inlays poured into its curly maple haft, the functional tomahawk sports a hand-forged 1080 carbon steel head with a smokable pipe later forge-welded onto the mild steel body.
(Caleb Royer image)

« PETER PRUYN
In the style of an 18th-century Indian khanjarli, the W2 fixed blade sports a more modern nickel silver guard and a coffin-style dyed giraffe bone handle.
(SharpByCoop image)

« TYLER TURNER
Like great gunsmiths, the maker checkered the walnut handle on his version of a dress kukri with a CPM-154 blade and nickel silver guard.
(SharpByCoop image)

⌃ J. ALEX RUIZ
An R.W. Loveless "Piker" tribute, the CPM 154 fixed blade employs black G-10 handle scales and 416 stainless bolsters. *(Caleb Royer image)*

STATE OF THE ART

Some people see beauty everywhere they go. It is an admirable quality and not as naïve or overly optimistic as some might believe. Beauty is all around us if only we take a moment to look and appreciate it. There might be places and situations that are not pretty or downright ugly, and that's life, but as the old saying goes, there's always a silver lining.

Many folks would not see beauty in steel, synthetic materials, leather, animal skin, shell, stone, resin or titanium. They might be inclined to scoff at artistic renderings on knives or sheaths. Knifemakers and embellishers are making every attempt to prove them wrong, and by the bevy of collectors jockeying for their art knives, they are making good headway in the fight against blade snobbery.

Some methods of knife embellishment are familiar to art aficionados—sculpting, engraving, carving and possibly even scrimshaw, to name a few. Others would come as a surprise, such as how blacksmiths forge damascus and mosaic damascus masterpieces or the way sheath makers use beading, engraving, stamping and carving in leather.

Maybe it is not so much seeing the beauty in the world but bringing what is pleasing forward from whatever materials one has on hand. The handcrafters whose work is featured herein make things beautiful. It is what they do.

Vivid Scrimshaw

DENNIS FRIEDLY
The maker left the stainless damascus to Mike Norris and the big cat scrimshaw on fossil walrus ivory to Linda Karst Stone.

(SharpByCoop image)

GAETAN BEAUCHAMP
A bear hunt plays out on the buffalo horn spacer of an oosic-handle damascus hunter that also comes with a frontier-style fringed leather sheath.

(SharpByCoop image)

JASON FRY
While the guard and spacers of the W2 "Cattle Drive Bowie" are fashioned from an 1889-1906 cemetery gate, an 1877 wrought iron railroad rail and an 1871 half dollar, the fossil walrus ivory handle is scrimshawed by Alice Carter in a cattle drive, church and cemetery motif.

(SharpByCoop image)

DENNIS FRIEDLY
A classic CPM-154 drop-point hunter is enlivened by Gil Rudolph engraving and Gary Williams scrimshaw in a salmon motif on ivory.

(SharpByCoop image)

GIL HIBBEN
Wolves scrimshawed by
Barbara Cullen peek out
from the wood handle of
a recurved fixed blade
with a hand guard.
(SharpByCoop image)

CLIFF PARKER
Are you hip to the hippo executed
by Roni Dietrich on the mammoth
ivory handle scales of an art
folder and again in the mosaic
damascus bolsters of the piece?
(SharpByCoop image)

DENNIS FRIEDLY
Rocky Mountain bighorn
sheep scrimshaw by Connie
Bellet jumps off the spaced stag
handle of an ATS-34 fixed-blade
hunter. *(SharpByCoop image)*

DENNIS FRIEDLY
A golden eagle is
brought to life by Connie
Bellet, framed in wood
and given a big hollow-
ground beak with a false
top edge to work with.
(SharpByCoop image)

That Gold Standard

If the value of these knives is directly linked to the gold within, they are pricy pieces of merchandise. Regardless of cost, high-end works of edged art are deserving of only the best, the cream of the crop, gold inlays and embellishments.

Many blade builders have backgrounds in jewelry making, and even those who do not can appreciate precious metals and the value they add to knives. Collectors gravitate toward dress daggers, folders and swords showcasing gold parts and inlays, and if a few jewels are thrown into the mix, all the better.

A king or queen does not step outside the castle without wearing the family jewels, after all, and perhaps a gold bracelet or pin. The crown might be left on the throne, but the robes are not worn plain without rings and jewelry. The mantle is not donned bare, and well-established tunics have gold thread as a basic form of dress.

Models herein are the gold standard of knives, and their value lies in what someone is willing to pony up for the precious pieces, in standard currency, trade, bitcoin or silver.

《 JAMIE LUNDELL
A "flowering vine" damascus talwar involves a steel, silver and gold hilt fashioned by Sandeep Singh Chauhan.
(SharpByCoop image)

» VAN BARNETT and DELLANA
Not ones to shy away from gold inlays, diamonds (160) and rubies, the duo did up a dress locking folder with Jason Morrissey damascus blade and black-lip pearl handle like only they could.

(SharpByCoop image)

« JOSH SMITH
A damascus dog bone bowie is done up in an African blackwood handle and 14k gold-domed pins.

(Eric Eggly, PointSeven image)

« KYLE ROYER
You see a lot of silver-wire wrapped handles, but rarely a sculpted and fluted carbon fiber grip with gold wire wrap, accompanied here by a deeply hollow-ground damascus blade, fuller and reinforced piercing tip.

(Caleb Royer image)

» DES HORN
Gold frames the mother-of-pearl handle of a Damasteel back-lock folder engraved and further gold-inlaid by Julien Marchal.
(BladeGallery.com image)

⌃ RICK DUNKERLEY
A golden line follows the folding damascus kris blade curves, while gold bolster borders and leaf engraving similarly highlight the art knife with a carved pearl handle.
(Eric Eggly, PointSeven image)

« VLADIMIR KOLENKO
Only sterling silver and gold would do for the mosaic damascus fixed dagger forged by Konstantin Lysenko.
(SharpByCoop image)

« BRUCE D. BUMP
The Han Dynasty Dragon Sword showcases a wax-cast stainless dragonhead pommel and guard with enough gold inlay and engraving to make the emperor drool, not to mention the mother-of-pearl hilt and two-foot damascus blade. *(Caleb Royer image)*

❥ HERUCUS BLOMERUS
Perhaps a first in flipper folders, the Damasteel piece combines a marbled carbon fiber handle with engraved and 24k-gold-inlaid bolsters. *(BladeGallery.com image)*

❯❯ DENNIS FRIEDLY
A CPM-154 New York Special is dressed up in a chrysocolla handle and a stainless guard featuring Ray Cover Jr. gold inlay and engraving.

(SharpByCoop image)

❮❮ LARRY NEWTON
As if one needs to say more than "18 diamonds set in a curved 14k-gold spacer," the symmetrical auto dagger also sports a damascus blade, mammoth ivory handle scales, a gold bale and bolsters inlaid with 24k-gold scrolls.

(SharpByCoop image)

❮❮ JOHNNY STOUT
When Alice Carter gold inlays and engraves knife bolsters, she puts prominent accents on form and flow, from the Bruce Bump "Eastwood" mosaic damascus blade to the bark mammoth ivory handle scales. *(Caleb Royer image)*

Insane Engraving

» KEVIN CASEY

Engraving can follow the flow of a piece or set it off. In the case of a feather damascus folder with mammoth ivory handle scales, the Joe Mason embellishment does both. *(SharpByCoop image)*

⌅ HERUCUS BLOMERUS

Engraved zirconium bolsters are the centerpiece of a Bohler M390 stainless flipper folder handled in marbled carbon fiber. *(BladeGallery. com image)*

« JOHNNY STOUT

The bolsters and backspacer of a Vaquero double-action auto are engraved by Wes Davis and combined with a Jerry Rados Turkish twist damascus blade and mammoth ivory handle scales. *(Caleb Royer image)*

« DENNIS FRIEDLY

"The End of the Trail" fighter, executed in Robert Eggerling damascus and bark mammoth ivory, is insanely engraved by Gil Rudolph to depict plains bison and a Native American facing a storm like neither had ever experienced. The bark mammoth ivory resembling the bison is secured with gold pins. *(SharpByCoop image)*

» SCOTT SAWBY
Few do it better than Ray Cover Jr. when it comes to engraving and gold inlaying wildlife onto the bolsters of dress locking folders, this one with a black nephrite jade handle and CPM-154 blade.

(SharpByCoop image)

« BILL RUPLE
For his dress slip-joint teardrop jackknife, the maker used CPM-154 blade steel, antique tortoiseshell handle slabs and gold-inlaying and engraving services of one Joe Mason.

(SharpByCoop image)

» BRUCE BARNETT
After the maker fashioned a pearl-handled feather damascus sowbelly, Diane Scalese took a graver to it with spectacular results.

(SharpByCoop image)

⌃ JIM POOR
I'd say it's a "Fancy Bull Cutter," done up here in a feather damascus blade and a 1075 handle frame fully and florally engraved by Sam Gooding.

(SharpByCoop image)

STATE OF THE ART

⌃ JOHN YOUNG
The maker gave Julie Warenski a guard and sub-hilt to engrave on his CPM-154 fighter featuring sambar stag handle scales.
(SharpByCoop image)

⌃ RICK DUNKERLEY
Build an interframe mosaic-damascus folder featuring black-lip pearl inlays surrounded by scroll and leaf engraving, and they will come.
(BladeGallery.com image)

⌃ TYLER TURNER
A dress slip-joint folder is done up in one CPM-154 blade, vintage ivory Micarta handle scales, a black G-10 shield and bolster engraving by Evan Watson.
(SharpByCoop image)

⌃ CURT ERICKSON
The stone handle, pointed pommel, and tightly patterned damascus blade is engulfed in Julie Warenski-Erickson gold inlay and engraving. *(Eric Eggly, PointSeven image)*

《 TIM BRITTON
When you want the Paul Markow engraving to stand out, you give the long-pull jackknife a pearl handle and little gold pins for accents.
(SharpByCoop image)

《 MATT HUMPHREYS
Engraving gives the long, wood-handle damascus fighter more oomph than it already has. *(Eric Eggly, PointSeven image)*

》 VINCE EVANS
A ladder-pattern damascus Schiavona sword showcases an insanely engraved steel basket with gold accents and a reeded blackwood hilt.
(SharpByCoop image)

YUPENG ZHAO
With engraved guard and frame, the "Outrage" pearl-handled CPM-3V push dagger is outrageous.

(SharpByCoop image)

GARY STEWART
A female vampire goes for the jugular on the front bolster, while the bluest of eyes overlook Transylvania on the opposite side of a mammoth ivory-handle Alabama damascus dagger. Tim Herman is the sure hand who engraved the piece.

(BladeGallery.com image))

H.H. FRANK
The engraved 14k-gold bolsters and tool steel blade of the dress locking folder are as exquisite as the mother-of-pearl handle scales.

(SharpByCoop image)

JERRY MCCLURE
Between black-lip mother-of-pearl and damascus is a touch of engraving in just the right spot.

(Caleb Royer image)

PHIL DUNN
Prickly pear hand engraving adorns the stainless bolsters of a CPM-154 dress slip-joint folder in amber-dyed, carved bone handle slabs.
(SharpByCoop image)

JONNY WALKER NILSSON
Detailed engraving spans the reindeer antler handle and sheath of the Sami style half-horn hunter outfitted with a Mattias Styrefors multi-bar composite damascus blade and a masur birch spacer.
(BladeGallery.com image)

PAR BJORKMAN
Though the insane engraving is seemingly in minutia, the folder with gold tab lock is a looker alright.
(Caleb Royer image)

SHAUN and SHARLA HANSEN
Tonight's highlight reel includes raised 24k gold, ruby, diamond and sapphire inlays, Bulino portrait engraving, sculpting, abalone inlays and the makers' own multi-bar composite damascus blade with a gold-inlaid core.
(SharpByCoop image)

⌃ **WILL ADKINS**

A dress locking folder, designed by William Evans, enlists a mirror-polished "Bjorkmans Twist" Damasteel blade, mother-of-pearl handle scales and zirconium bolsters engraved by Evan Watson.

(SharpByCoop image

⌃ **TOM PLOPPERT**

The most handsome "Cowboy Cutter" on the range, the feather damascus piece is forged by Andrew Smith and showcases a jigged pre-ban elephant ivory handle and 416 stainless bolsters engraved and gold inlaid by Joe Mason.

(SharpByCoop image)

⌃ **NEELS ROOS**

The flats and bolsters of a 12C27 drop-point hunter are engraved to represent the Mayan god, Itzamna, complemented by an African blackwood handle.

(BladeGallery.com image)

⌃ **ANDREW GARRETT**

An Australian landscape is etched and engraved onto the 1075 blade of a custom bowie with a ringed Gidgee handle.

(SharpByCoop image)

» ANDRE THORBURN
A satin-finished CTS-XHP stainless folder showcases textured, engraved and heat-colored zirconium bolsters and a nickel wire carbon fiber handle.
(BladeGallery.com image)

« ANDREW LEE ADAMS
The Protech Brend 3 Auto has a damascus blade, black-lip pearl push button and a solid 416 stainless handle engraved and gold inlaid by Andrew Lee Adams.
(Caleb Royer image)

« STANLEY BUZEK
A Texas trapper parades Randy Haas "Reverb"-pattern damascus, interior mammoth ivory and Alice Carter gold inlay and engraving.
(SharpByCoop image)

⌃ MATTHEW BERRY
Featuring a K.C. Lund damascus blade, the "Valsgarde Grave 5 Sword" is decked out in a black cherry burl hilt and an engraved and pierced bronze guard and pommel inlaid with garnets and bone.
(SharpByCoop image)

⌃ BURT FLANAGAN
Inlaying the pearl handle of the interframe CPM-154 folder with abalone was as inspired as commissioning Alice Carter to gold inlay and engrave the piece.
(SharpByCoop image)

Handle Craft

Handle with care and cut with aplomb, for these are the handcrafted cutters of the 21st century. With so much care given to forged blades—whether mono-steel, san mai or damascus—and the stock-removal method of blade building, the makers of the knives on this and the following pages reason that just as much attention should be afforded the handle halves.

Seriously, it is incredible what knifemakers can do through carving, sculpting, stacking, inlaying and manipulating handle materials. Plus, bringing out some of the natural beauty of wood, shell, ivory and pearl allows for a dizzying array of aesthetically pleasing grips from which to choose.

Handle craft is alive and well in the knife industry, displayed here in all its glory, yet another example of form meeting function and art going hand in hand (or hand in handle) with utility. Knifemakers never cease to amaze.

《 JOE FAUSONE
The cholla cactus handle with turquoise inlays is nicely done on an AEB-L chef's knife.
(Caleb Royer image)

《 BRIAN TIGHE
The material choice is sometimes half the battle. Here a purple and black FatCarbon carbon-fiber composite handle for a Damasteel chef's knife.
(BladeGallery.com image)

⌃ RON APPLETON
The anodized titanium frame of the S7 "Angel Infilock 2.0" folder is skillfully and gorgeously machined from one piece of material.
(SharpByCoop image)

⌃ ANTON VAN DER WESTHUIZEN
To go with the Bertie Rietveld "Nebula" damascus blade, the maker fashioned a tri-pocket titanium handle with Timascus inlays.
(BladeGallery.com image)

⌃ MATTHEW BERRY
An entirely impressive Anglo-Saxon ring-hilt sword dons a 30-inch Emiliano Carrillo damascus blade, and a bronze, silver and horn hilt with mosaic pommel inlays.
(SharpByCoop image)

⌃ DAVID LISCH
Talk about handle craft! The damascus knife has a latch at the back that, when opened, allows the stag grip to come off. *(Eric Eggly, PointSeven image)*

⌃ ANDRE THORBURN
The Damasteel flipper folder hits its stride in a gold-leaf shred carbon fiber handle and engraved and gold-inlaid zirconium bolsters. *(BladeGallery.com image)*

» DELLANA
A sterling silver and 14k-gold bolster is the star of the dress locking liner folder in a ladder-pattern damascus blade and black-lip pearl handle. *(SharpByCoop image)*

⌄ RICK DUNKERLEY
The combination of engraved bolsters and carved antique tortoiseshell handle scales makes for one killer composite damascus Wharncliffe folder.
(BladeGallery.com image)

⌃ JACKSON RUMBLE
An integral keyhole-style bowie-fighter is given a 5160 blade and desert ironwood grip.
(Caleb Royer Image)

⌃ MORGAN AXELSSON
What's not going on within the confines of the crosscut mammoth ivory and masur birch handle, complete with teardrop-shaped blue opal inlay? Then there is that multi-bar mosaic damascus blade forged by Henry Hilden.
(BladeGallery.com image)

» VAN BARNETT
The damascus fighter's suit of armor was the envy of the kingdom, made from bronze, carbon fiber and blued steel. *(SharpByCoop image)*

» JAY REPLOGLE
No ordinary bog oak handle (or damascus bowie, for that matter), the piece is carved and features a sculpted sterling silver guard and garnet and ruby inlays.
(SharpByCoop image)

» DENNIS FRIEDLY
Fully engraved and gold inlaid by Gil Rudolph, this masterpiece showcases a Robert Eggerling damascus blade and a jewelry polymer handle, as well as amethyst and rubies thrown in for good measure.
(SharpByCoop image)

« LLOYD HALE
He pieced together the abalone and pearl handle of a 440C bowie with the precision of a surgeon and the eye of an artist.
(SharpByCoop image)

⌃ MARDI MESHEJIAN
Sometimes, it is not as much about the materials— damascus, titanium, copper and marbled carbon fiber—as it is how you use them.
(SharpByCoop image)

» ALAN MITCHELL
Who says you can't look by feeling? Imagine gripping the African blackwood handle wrapped in twisted wire, running your index finger up onto the textured bronze bolster and lightly thumbing the edge of that Tinus Steenkamp san mai blade, just to check for sharpness.

« GEORGE MULLER
Mammoth ivory and Gibeon meteorite inlays grace the copper wire-infused carbon fiber handle of a Damasteel flipper folder.
(BladeGallery.com image)

» STEVEN RAMOS
What's sexier, the serpentine CTS-XHP blade with a deep, hollow grind, or the genuine Epidote and quartz gemstone handle? *(Caleb Royer image)*

NEELS VAN DEN BERG
A twist-pattern damascus stiletto dons an antique bronze handle with brass accents. *(BladeGallery.com image)*

BILL BEHNKE
The full-tang damascus integral showcases a G-Carta handle—a composite of natural fibers and fabrics mixed with epoxy under pressure and heat. *(Eric Eggly, PointSeven image)*

PAUL DISTEFANO
A "Day of the River" bowie boasts a mosaic damascus blade, blackened mild steel guard with gold "wings," and African blackwood handle carved in a river motif with a koi fish which, after 100 years of perseverance, reached the top of the waterfall and was turned into a golden dragon as a reward from the gods. *(SharpByCoop image)*

CORY MARTIN
"Lagoon Creature" comes to life via hand-carved, heat-colored titanium, damascus and copper. *(Cory Martin Imaging)*

DARRIEL CASTON
There's more than one way to dress up a titanium handle, as shown on the Vegas Forge Damascus slip-joint folder. *(SharpByCoop image)*

ANDREW MEERS
Just wow—where to start, let's see, a W2 push dagger blade with smoky temper line, the skeletonized and artistically contoured and colored African blackwood handle and frame, or the little glass vial at the top center of the grip that contains garnets? *(SharpByCoop image)*

» CHARL PIENAAR
Like the boss it is, a Bohler M390 stainless front flipper folder takes on a bead-blasted titanium handle with a brass-flake forged carbon fiber front scale. *(BladeGallery.com image)*

⌄ LUKE HAAG
The carbon fiber, steel and beryllium copper handle with pointed pommel would deal a blow, not to mention the hollow-ground, recurved 5160 blade. *(Caleb Royer image)*

⌃ DAN BIDINGER
Attention was paid to the contoured green canvas Micarta and bloodwood handle half of the satin-finished O1 chef's knife.
(BladeGallery.com image)

⌃ MATT PARKINSON
The chef and paring knives sport Damasteel blades and NuGold-inlaid curly maple handles depicting the Cajun trinity—onions, bell peppers and celery—and root vegetables.
(SharpByCoop image)

« JOE EDSON
A high-performance chef's knife is enabled by a san mai blade, stacked Micarta bolster and "starry night" G-carta handle. *(BladeGallery.com image)*

⌃ FOREST "BUTCH" SHEELY
At 15.5 inches overall, there was plenty of room on the 1095 camp knife for some silver wire inlay on the curly maple spacers of an antler handle. *(Eric Eggly, PointSeven image)*

» JIM ARBUCKLE
Not only is the handle of the 154CM Nakiri vegetable cleaver contoured snakeskin sycamore, but the spine also features bamboo file work that has been filled with black epoxy and polished, so no food particles become lodged in the crevices. *(BladeGallery.com image)*

« ANDREAS KALANI
While the 1095 blade is electro mirror polished, the "Natural Galaxy" handle encompasses Middle Eastern turquoise and flowers. *(SharpByCoop image)*

» MATTHEW GASKILL
Ivory paper Micarta bolsters, and a Tasmanian blackwood handle with Westinghouse Micarta liners are a good look on a 13-inch 1095 fixed blade. *(Eric Eggly, PointSeven image)*

» WES LYONS
Combining EDC feather damascus by Gary Ellis Jr. and hybrid handle scales of stabilized Vasticola burl (eucalyptus) and clear resin, the maker created a masterpiece. *(Caleb Royer image)*

» SHANE TAYLOR
Not many makers would think to combine blued sambar stag, forged bronze (in a skull motif) and niter-blued screws for the handle of a damascus fighter, but more should. *(BladeGallery.com image)*

⌂ RANDY LEE
An 11-layer stacked handle defines the CPM-154 sub-hilt fighter, with materials including ironwood, amber, Kirinite, acrylic and Micarta. *(BladeGallery.com image)*

» ABEL PRICE
It's how the maker shaped and stippled the African blackwood handle with copper and deer antler spacers that sets off the grip of an AEB-L "Deco Petty" model.
(SharpByCoop image)

⏷ MICHAEL ZIEBA
Silver koi fish swim in a sea of titanium and bronze on a "Thor" Damasteel flipper folder.
(SharpByCoop image)

« MARK KNAPP
Golden engraving highlights the mammoth tooth and musk ox horn handle of a choice damascus hunting knife. The maker fashioned his own sheath for the piece, and why not?!
(SharpByCoop image)

« A2—ANDRE VAN HEERDEN and ANDRE THORBURN
A san mai damascus blade working off a ceramic IKBS (Ikoma Korth Bearing System) is accompanied by a titanium handle creatively inlaid with snakeskin carbon fiber. *(BladeGallery.com image)*

« GREGER FORSELIUS
There is no doubt the Mattias Styrefors multi-bar mosaic damascus blade is a looker, but likewise the mammoth ivory and green birch handle.
(BladeGallery.com image)

⏶ ALEXANDER NOOT
To complement the forged-to-shape Japanese-style san mai blade with a white paper core, the maker fashioned a bronze, tagua nut, snakewood and stabilized bog oak handle fastened by a simple mosaic pin. *(Caleb Royer image)*

≫ DENIS BUDAK

Details made on the maker's Deckel Pantograph include mother-of-pearl inlays within the Timascus handle scales, a damascus "superstar" inlay on the pivot head, a one-hand-opening thumb groove along the Damasteel blade and more. *(Caleb Royer image)*

≫ JERRY GOETTIG

The handle of the 8-inch AEB-L chef's knife is Fordite set on grey G-10, with Fordite being paint layers from old Ford and other automotive plants. *(BladeGallery.com image)*

≪ E. JAY HENDRICKSON

Silver vines and textured leaves are inlaid into the curly maple handle of a hand-forged 80CrV2 clip-point hunter that has an India stag pommel. *(BladeGallery.com image)*

≫ VLADIMIR KOLENKO

Rich in inlays, embellishments and skilled craftsmanship, the handle of the Turkish twist damascus dagger features sterling silver, 14-karat gold, mother-of-pearl and garnets.

(SharpByCoop image)

⋓ WILLEM STEENKAMP

An eye for style is evident via the burgundy Micarta handle with damascus shield and Westinghouse Micarta bolster of the RWL-34 slip joint folder.

(BladeGallery.com image)

≫ JAVAN ROBERTS

The CPM S110V "Mariko" fighter features a brass bolster and spruced up, inlaid and rubberized carbon fiber handle.

(SharpByCoop image)

Sharp-Dressed Daggers

» GARY LANGLEY
A tightly patterned damascus dagger is done up in blued steel fittings and a natural handle aged gracefully. *(Eric Eggly PointSeven image)*

⌄ SCOTT GALLAGHER
A European quillon dagger is done up in a mosaic damascus blade and guard, and a gold wire-wrapped, fluted African blackwood handle. *(SharpByCoop image)*

⌃ ADAM BALKOVIC
A mother-of-pearl inlay within the carbon fiber handle provides a window into the soul of the blackened, hollow-ground CPM-3V dagger with a spear point. *(SharpByCoop image)*

» MIKE J. O'BRIEN
A mortised-tang dagger is presented in a hand-rubbed and finished CPM-154 blade, a sculpted 416 stainless guard and a stabilized curly Koa handle. *(SharpByCoop image)*

JONNY KABLE
A multi-bar damascus dagger gets it done in a gun-blued mild steel guard and pommel and an ebony handle.
(BladeGallery.com image)

JEREMY YELLE
The W1 fighter features a "no clay hamon [temper line]," African blackwood handle, and forged and textured copper fittings with a stainless steel spacer.
(Caleb Royer image)

A. BRETT SCHALLER
The curvy kris dagger is done up in CPM-154 steel, nickel silver, green-dyed box elder burl and a sterling silver twisted-wire handle wrap. *(SharpByCoop image)*

RICHARD DAWES
A pyrite sphere trapped in the crown pommel gives the "Fool's Dagger" its name, while the Devin Thomas damascus blade and gold wire-wrapped, fluted mammoth ivory handle give it game.
(SharpByCoop image)

» MATTHEW JAYNES
Three groovily ground, double-edged daggers sport W2 blades, G-10 handles, leather sheaths and other amenities.

(SharpByCoop image)

» JOHN YOUNG
The mirror-polished CPM-154 dagger poses in a Picasso marble handle and a gun-blued steel guard.

(BladeGallery.com image)

⌃ KELLY VERMEER-VELLA
Not just the guard stands out on the ring dagger, but also the damascus blade and sterling silver wire-wrapped, fluted African blackwood handle.

(SharpByCoop image)

« MACE VITALE and BILLY MACE IMEL
With both makers' first and middle names being "William Mace," they decided to toast the occasion by making a dagger. Mace Vitale forged the damascus blade, which was ground by Billy Mace Imel and then finished by Vitale.

(SharpByCoop image)

STUART SMITH
The carved African blackwood handle creates the illusion of a braided leather wrap on a forged and satin-finished 5160 dagger.
(BladeGallery.com image)

PEKKA TUOMINEN
The sleek "Protector" (Suojaleijee) dagger is dressed in an African blackwood handle, nickel silver guard and a 15N20, 184 and 80CrV2 damascus blade.
(SharpByCoop image)

BILL POOR
The wood-handle dog-bone dagger was destined for damascus greatness.
(Eric Eggly, PointSeven image)

JOSH SMITH
Four-bar "W's"-pattern composite damascus and carved walrus ivory are but two amenities of the take-down art dagger that comes with a Wilburn Forge and Leather sheath.
(SharpByCoop image)

» YUPENG ZHAO

The appropriately named "Unicorn" dagger (Is it real?) is ground from a single piece of ATS-34 steel after heat treatment and outfitted with a mother-of-pearl handle.

(Caleb Royer image)

⩗ JAVAN ROBERTS

The maker enlisted Alabama damascus, copper and antique Micarta for his "Anjin" fixed-blade fighter.

(SharpByCoop image)

⌃ PAUL DISTEFANO

The maker's first dagger, "Flora," won the "Best Handle Design" award at the 2021 ICCE Show for its carved woolly mammoth ivory handle, not to mention that mosaic damascus blade and sculpted damascus guard.

(SharpByCoop image)

《 ANDREW MEERS

Embellished from tip to pommel, the "Vulpecula" dagger displays a 1080-and-15N20 damascus blade, an African blackwood handle, gold accents and a glass vial holding a fox tooth in the center of it all.

(SharpByCoop image)

» DON FOGG
The "Life and Death" dagger blade is pattern-welded with high texture on one side (death) and a cathedral pattern (life) on the other side. The handle is ebony, silver, gold and boulder pearl, and the knife portrays the duality of life with pairs of opposites—life/death, good/evil and beauty/ugliness. The life side shows an orchid and an opal, representing light. The death side showcases a demon with the ebony handle pierced in a disturbing, chaotic manner, revealing the textured blade tang below.

« BOB APPLEBY
A clean Randall-styled 2-8 dagger enlists a mirror-polished 440C blade, stainless guard, S-grade resin ivory handle and an aluminum pommel.
(SharpByCoop image)

⌃ JOHN APRIL
The offset almost pistol grip-like snakewood handle, with red G-10 liners and a black linen Micarta frame, is just so cool on a CPM-154 push dagger.
(SharpByCoop image)

« AARON WILBURN
Two Turkish twists and two Firestorm damascus bars make up the blade of the fixed dagger with a wrought iron clamshell guard and a mammoth ivory grip.
(SharpByCoop image)

« PAUL SAVAGE
One classy ring dagger is delivered in a foot-long damascus blade, buffalo horn handle and blued stainless fittings. *(Eric Eggly PointSeven image)*

Custom Carry Pieces

Knives in display cases are nice when company arrives for dinner, and the conversation centers around interior home décor, furnishings, accent pieces and collectibles within the house. Guests would be more than impressed with any of the blades on this and the following pages, resting on stands, behind glass, on velvet slipcases or microfiber cloths.

That is great and admirable, but knives are meant to be carried and used. Not all knives need to look black, tactical or ready for the hunt or pack. Some can be fancy pieces with high-end materials, designs and details. There is nothing wrong with looking good while working, and the custom carry pieces herein are adept at both.

Makers are not fashioning works of art that will not cut or cut it in the real world. Anyone who has attended a handmade knife show or talked with any of the renowned knifemakers worldwide quickly realizes that the vast majority take their work seriously. They test blades, pride themselves in the fine fit and finishes of every piece they make and have no room for wiggle or wobble. They make custom carry pieces meant to be toted, used and cared for as the tools of the trade that they are.

》 STANLEY BUZEK
There is so much to like about the Texas trapper—the engraved and gold-inlaid bolsters by Alice Carter, the Randy Haas "Reverb"-pattern damascus blades and the bark mammoth ivory handle scales.
(SharpByCoop image)

《 ANDRE THORBURN
Built with a Damasteel blade and blue lightning strike carbon fiber handle scales, the folder shows off engraved and gold-inlaid zirconium bolsters.
(BladeGallery.com image)

《 JULIAN ANTUNES
Three hundred layers of damascus and a gold spacer set the tone for a fixed-blade utility knife featuring a black ash burl handle.
(SharpByCoop image)

» BRIAN BROWN
The lava field-like frame of the Damasteel Taka v2 flipper folder is Chad Nichols four-alloy DarkTi. *(SharpByCoop image)*

» DARRIEL CASTON
The California-legal auto has a deeply etched blade and handle in a skulls-and-crossbones motif.
(SharpByCoop image)

⌃ ANDREW FRANKLAND
A 3-inch gent's side knife will slide into the sheath silently and go along for the ride.

« DAVE SKINNER
The hand-forged damascus fixed blade with Chittum burl handle comes complete with a tooled custom leather sheath.
(BladeGallery.com image)

« MIKE TYRE
Of sole authorship, the low-layer, multi-bar Turkish twist damascus folder showcases black-lip mother-of-pearl handle scales. *(Eric Eggly, PointSeven image)*

RICK DUNKERLEY

While the damascus for the blade and handle is forged to resemble a slow-moving stream, the gold inlay and engraving in the middle of it all make for the prettiest island this side of Bora Bora.

(BladeGallery.com image)

NATHAN CAROTHERS

So that you can handily tote the CPM-3V "Field Knife 2" with a grooved cocobolo handle, the maker asked Paul Long to fashion a basketweave-style leather sheath for the piece.

(SharpByCoop image)

ANDERS HOGSTROM

A marriage of Nordic and Russian styles, the TAGA Kwaiken utility belt knife is outfitted in a double-edged 1050 carbon steel blade with hamon (temper line), textured bronze fittings and a fossil walrus ivory handle.

(Mitchell D. Cohen Photography)

CHRIS SHARP

The maker pierced the shield and vintage paper Micarta handle of a damascus single-blade trapper.

(SharpByCoop image)

CURT THOMPSON

The "Trail Boss" calls the shots using a CPM-154 blade, nickel silver guard and a pre-1972 walrus ivory tusk handle. Claude Scott fashioned an ostrich skin-inlaid, lined leather sheath for the piece.

(SharpByCoop image)

« FRANCOIS DU TOIT
Supplied with a padded pouch, a Damasteel flipper folder sports matching bolsters and shred carbon fiber handle scales.

(BladeGallery.com image)

» ANDREA LISCH
The definition of utilitarian art, the knife features a hand-forged damascus blade with integral bolster and a presentation-grade black and white ebony handle.

(BladeGallery.com image)

⌣ GABRIEL MABRY
With a name like the "Beagle V1 Belt Knife," one must take pride in carrying the antique-finished 80CrV2 fixed blade handled in tigerwood.

(BladeGallery.com image)

» KEVIN CASEY
Feather damascus, bronze and fossil walrus ivory lend flavor to a fixed-blade bowie. *(SharpByCoop image)*

» JIM PROVOST
He calls it a "Hidden Bowie Knife," perhaps because the Damasteel piece with Asian satinwood handle fits so snugly in its leather sheath (or perhaps because the tang is hidden).

(SharpByCoop image)

» GEORGE MULLER
Imagine busting out his "Hakkapella"-pattern Damasteel flipper folder in a carbon fiber handle with meteorite and abalone shell inlays to slice a thread or two.
(BladeGallery.com image)

« ANDREW LEE ADAMS
Taking customization to a new level, the Protech Godfather Auto is engraved, inlaid with gold and rubies, given a Damasteel blade and outfitted with ancient mastodon molar handle scales.
(Caleb Royer image)

» TIM ROBERTSON
A dress slip-joint folder is outfitted in a CPM-154 blade, a stainless frame with integral bolsters and red stag handle scales.
(SharpByCoop image)

⌃ MIKE WALTON
The maker's first knife is a Bob Lum-inspired dress utility piece in a CPM-154 blade, desert ironwood handle and Paul Long sheath.
(SharpByCoop image)

« DENNIS FRIEDLY
Imagine carrying the gent's lock-back folder outfitted in a Robert Eggerling mosaic damascus blade, gold-lip pearl handle and Chris Meyer gold-inlaid and engraved bolsters.
(SharpByCoop image)

« DON HANSON III
The trapper sports a W2 blade, stainless bolsters and a stag handle.
(SharpByCoop image)

▼ TREVOR BURGER
Damasteel stainless damascus bolsters are inlaid into each side of the lighting strike carbon fiber handle scales of a spear-point M390 stainless folder. *(BladeGallery.com image)*

▼ PETER MARTIN
The blue lightning strike carbon-fiber handle scales and "Zirco-Ti" bolsters are the suit and tie of a Damasteel flipper folder.
(Cory Martin Imaging)

» PRINCETON WONG
Inspired by Japanese design and wing geometries, the Damasteel flipper folder parades a Timascus handle, zirconium inlays and silver bolsters.
(Eric Eggly, PointSeven image)

« STEVE SKIFF
It's nice to have an Accomplice … flipper folder, particularly one in a Damasteel blade, black Timascus bolster and 3D milled titanium handle.
(BladeGallery.com image)

⌃ TOBIN HILL
Touches such as fluted bolsters, ancient woolly mammoth ivory handle scales and file-worked CPM-154 blades make it a primo piece. *(BladeGallery.com image)*

DAN BIDINGER
Not too many makers offer Persian field knives like this 80CrV2 high carbon piece in green and black Micarta. *(BladeGallery.com image)*

JESSICA BURKE
The locking-liner folder features a matching feather-pattern damascus blade and handle along with a faceted sapphire thumb stud. *(BladeGallery.com image)*

JOHNNY STOUT
Ingredients of the flavorful folder include bolsters engraved and gold inlaid by Alice Carter, including baked-on glass enamel flowers, a black-lip mother-of-pearl handle and a Doug Ponzio Turkish twist damascus blade. *(Caleb Royer image)*

TYLER TURNER
The contrast between the mother-of-pearl handle and blackened O1 tool steel blade, separated by Evan Watson engraved bolsters, works beautifully on a Texas trapper. *(SharpByCoop image)*

AARON WILBURN
A flame touches the jigged black paper Micarta handle of the "Dino Slipjoint," that of the CPM-154 stainless kind. *(BladeGallery.com image)*

J.D. VAN DEVENTER
With the Damasteel blade working off two tracks of ball bearings, the flipper folder action is as silky smooth as that Fat Carbon "lava flow" handle. *(BladeGallery.com image)*

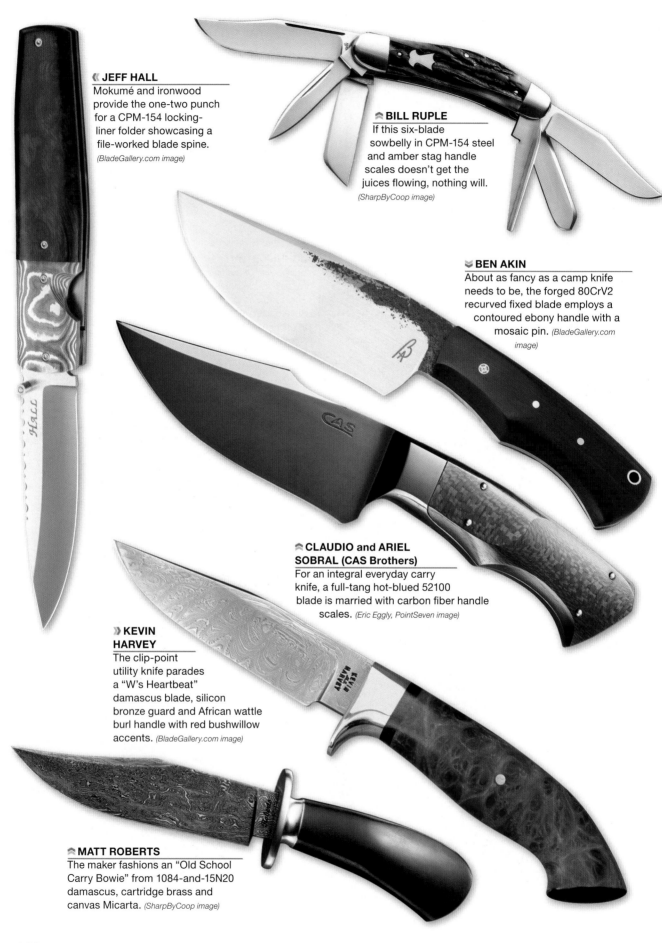

JEFF HALL
Mokumé and ironwood provide the one-two punch for a CPM-154 locking-liner folder showcasing a file-worked blade spine. *(BladeGallery.com image)*

BILL RUPLE
If this six-blade sowbelly in CPM-154 steel and amber stag handle scales doesn't get the juices flowing, nothing will. *(SharpByCoop image)*

BEN AKIN
About as fancy as a camp knife needs to be, the forged 80CrV2 recurved fixed blade employs a contoured ebony handle with a mosaic pin. *(BladeGallery.com image)*

CLAUDIO and ARIEL SOBRAL (CAS Brothers)
For an integral everyday carry knife, a full-tang hot-blued 52100 blade is married with carbon fiber handle scales. *(Eric Eggly, PointSeven image)*

KEVIN HARVEY
The clip-point utility knife parades a "W's Heartbeat" damascus blade, silicon bronze guard and African wattle burl handle with red bushwillow accents. *(BladeGallery.com image)*

MATT ROBERTS
The maker fashions an "Old School Carry Bowie" from 1084-and-15N20 damascus, cartridge brass and canvas Micarta. *(SharpByCoop image)*

» HERUCUS BLOMERUS
A custom flipper folder sports a Chad Nichols SG2 Takefu blade and a full-scale, raindrop-pattern MokuTi handle with silver inlay.
(SharpByCoop image)

⌄ STEVE VANDERKOLFF
The slip-joint folder's red lace agate handle is an attention grabber, married to a CPM 154 blade that works off the Dellana dot grip system. *(Eric Eggly, PointSeven image)*

« DANIEL GUTIERREZ
The classy fixed blade is fashioned from acid-etched 80CrV2 steel, canvas Micarta bolsters and a Honduran rosewood handle.
(Caleb Royer image)

« DES HORN
A Damasteel flipper folder benefits from lightning strike carbon fiber handle scales, blue-anodized and file-worked titanium liners, and titanium damascus bolsters.
(BladeGallery.com image)

« JIM TURECEK
Not just the carved oosic handles are fancy, but the thumb studs, damascus blades and file work, as well. *(SharpByCoop image)*

⌄ A2—ANDRE VAN HEERDEN and ANDRE THORBURN
Take a san mai damascus blade with an SG2 powdered metallurgical stainless core, add a crosscut copper "snakeskin" handle by Fat Carbon, and you have a fine, fancy flipper folder.
(BladeGallery.com image)

Mosaic
Manipulation

I s a person still considered a blacksmith if they combine alloys for knife blades, arrange them in a manner in which they can create images, repeatable patterns and geometric designs, forge them together and etch the steel to bring out the artistic renderings? Or have they graduated to steel artisans, mosaic damascus smiths or master craftsmen?

It is akin to asking if a car customizer, detailer or pinstripe specialist is still an auto plant assembler. Is an architect a home builder, or an interior designer a painter? Now we are splitting hairs, but the point is made—when someone excels at a craft to the point of becoming specialized in that area, they deserve a little recognition.

The mosaic damascus blade manipulation paraded before readers on this page and those that follow is top-notch artistry by steel smiths who have mastered their crafts. They are still knifemakers, still blade forgers, still smiths, but also master craftsmen and women. They have graduated to new levels and deserve a little acknowledgment.

《 SCOTT GALLAGHER
"Brain freeze" mosaic damascus blows the mind, as do the hot-blued guard and dyed sambar stag handle of a D-guard bowie.
(SharpByCoop image)

MAREKO MAUMASI
The Gyuto is forged from "Maelstrom" mosaic damascus and features a forged integral bolster, recurved heel, a redwood burl handle and black G-10 and bronze spacers. *(SharpByCoop image)*

JAMIE LUNDELL
The maker was all in on the talwar when he forged a "key"-pattern mosaic damascus blade for the piece and then commissioned Sandeep Singh Chauhan to fashion a jaw-dropping gold, silver and steel hilt. *(SharpByCoop image)*

RICHARD PATTERSON
The knife that cut the maker's wedding cake showcases a mosaic damascus blade with an S-grind, and a stabilized, dyed curly maple handle. *(Caleb Royer image)*

BILL POOR
A shoutout to his home state of Texas, the maker forged a mosaic damascus blade for the beautiful bowie in a wood handle. *(Eric Eggly, PointSeven image)*

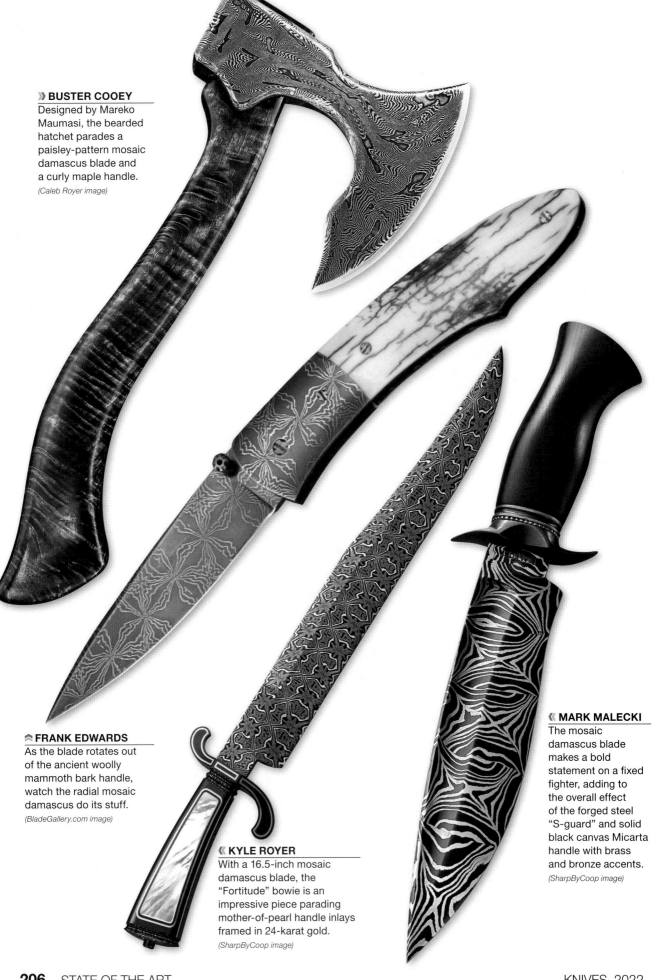

» BUSTER COOEY
Designed by Mareko Maumasi, the bearded hatchet parades a paisley-pattern mosaic damascus blade and a curly maple handle.
(Caleb Royer image)

⌃ FRANK EDWARDS
As the blade rotates out of the ancient woolly mammoth bark handle, watch the radial mosaic damascus do its stuff.
(BladeGallery.com image)

« KYLE ROYER
With a 16.5-inch mosaic damascus blade, the "Fortitude" bowie is an impressive piece parading mother-of-pearl handle inlays framed in 24-karat gold.
(SharpByCoop image)

« MARK MALECKI
The mosaic damascus blade makes a bold statement on a fixed fighter, adding to the overall effect of the forged steel "S-guard" and solid black canvas Micarta handle with brass and bronze accents.
(SharpByCoop image)

GREGER FORSELIUS
A Swedish long hunter makes good use of a Konstantin Lysenko multi-bar mosaic damascus blade, desert ironwood handle and mammoth ivory spacer. *(BladeGallery.com image)*

JUSTIN CHENAULT
An appealing mosaic damascus blade is complemented nicely by a fossilized walrus ivory handle. *(Eric Eggly, PointSeven image)*

MATTHEW PARKINSON
The kitchen knife set includes boning, carving and chef's knives in Koa wood handles, nickel silver bolsters and mouthwatering mosaic damascus blades. *(SharpByCoop image)*

ANDREW TAKACH
Like a canary, the 12-bar mosaic damascus bowie with sambar stag handle and blackened mild steel fittings sings a sweet tune. *(SharpByCoop image)*

» AARON WILBURN
An aptly named diamond mosaic blade beautifies a stag-handle bowie with wrought iron guard and butt cap, nickel silver trim and a bronze spacer.
(SharpByCoop image)

» KEN HALL
A mosaic damascus tanto combines a giraffe bone handle with a copper tsuba (guard) and stainless, red paper and copper spacers.
(SharpByCoop image)

⩔ C. LUIS PINA
An 8.25-inch chef's knife is made from an old family recipe of hand-forged mosaic damascus and quilted maple burl.
(BladeGallery.com image)

⩗ JOSH FISHER
With a checkered grip and tightly patterned mosaic damascus blade, the fighter is a prize.
(Caleb Royer image)

» MIKE TYRE
Mosaic "snowflakes" damascus and black-lip mother-of-pearl enliven a coke bottle pattern pocketknife featuring a peridot-inlaid thumb stud. *(Eric Eggly, PointSeven image)*

« JIM POOR
If you are pining for pinecone damascus, you have come to the right place—a dress locking folder with mammoth ivory handle scales. *(SharpByCoop image)*

» JASON ELLARD
If you can get past the "dragon's breath" mosaic feather damascus blade, you'll notice a dyed and stabilized maple burl handle. *(SharpByCoop image)*

« NEELS ROOS
The mosaic blade and bolsters of the art folder, forged by Ettore Gianferrari, have a crystalline-like aesthetic to them, complemented by a verdite handle. *(BladeGallery.com image)*

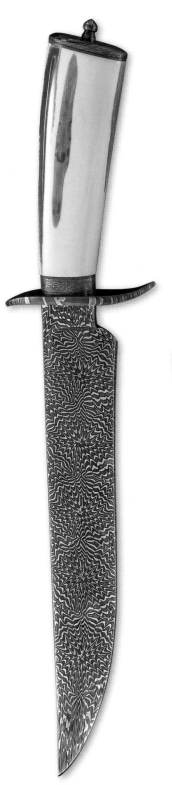

⌃ **STEVE RANDALL**
The maker's first foray into mosaic damascus is a smashing success, here on a bowie knife with coined titanium spacers and a fossil walrus ivory handle.
(SharpByCoop image)

⌃ **LEO POTTER**
The tile mosaic damascus blade and bolster are mated with a Bethlehem olivewood handle, a rust-blued spacer and nickel silver pin. *(Caleb Royer image)*

⌃ **JOSH WISOR**
The maker's take on a Persian-style fighter has a wicked mosaic damascus blade, a blackened antiqued bronze guard, and a carved ringed Gidgee handle.
(SharpByCoop image)

⌃ **DIONATAM FRANCO**
The mosaic damascus blade pattern is so tightly woven that it equates to being the satin or silk of buckeye burl-handle chef's knives. *(BladeGallery. com image)*

⌃ ANDERS HOGSTROM and CONNY PERSSON

The only bowie the makers have built together, "The Crag" features a five-bar "explosion," twist and "zig-zag" mosaic damascus blade, an antiqued and textured sterling silver guard and a fossil walrus ivory handle left natural at the end.

(SharpByCoop image)

⌃ JORDAN LAMOTHE

The maker forged one stunning mosaic damascus blade for his chef's knife handled in bog oak, mammoth tooth, silver and meteorite.

(SharpByCoop image)

⌃ SHANE TAYLOR

Shane figured, if he was forging two-bar mosaic damascus anyway, he might as well make it into an 18.2-inch "Dragon Wing Khuki Bat" inspired by Gurkha kukris and including a forged dragon-wing bronze guard and contoured black and white ebony handle. *(BladeGallery. com image)*

⌃ SCOTT JORAM SWEDER

The mosaic twist damascus bowie blade is 10 inches long with fittings of explosion damascus and a handle from mammoth ivory and African blackwood.

(Caleb Royer image)

Sheath
Beauty

I t seems there is no such thing as a plain leather or Kydex sheath anymore, but instead, knifemakers and their commissioned leatherworkers ply their trades in multi-media handcraft. Modern leather sheaths are mostly tooled, carved and inlaid with various pelts, skins and other natural and synthetic materials.

Fringed leather, horsehair and beads make appearances, as do such inlaid embellishments as jewels, damascus, abalone and pearl.

Each sheath is stitched, molded and crafted with care. Snaps, loops and frog closures are standard, but many knives are held snug via leather molded around guards, bolsters and blades.

A knife case, wood scabbard or simple leather slip sheath would protect edges. Still, it is the artistry in combination with utilitarian aspects of sheaths that make them beautiful and beneficial to the sale. It is sheath beauty, and there is no denying the appeal.

》 **KEVIN CASEY**
Feather damascus blades and fossil ivory handles deserve Larry Parson inlaid snap sheaths to be worn on the belt, where they can be admired.
(SharpByCoop image)

KENNETH WEBB

Sometimes, the sheath for a mosaic damascus Gyuto model should be stabilized white oak, and so it is. The knife sports a nickel silver bolster, Mokume gane spacer and stabilized ziricote handle.

(Caleb Royer image)

STEVEN RAMOS

The perfect home for a recurved CPM 154 fixed blade with a Cave Creek Jasper handle, the sheath is genuine shark skin inlaid in hand-stitched leather.

(Caleb Royer image)

JULIAN ANTUNES

Sheath fashioner Paul Long knows how to make a knife feel at home.

(SharpByCoop image)

KEN HALL
The maker of the curly Koa-handle fighter with an arrowhead-shaped keyhole-style blackwood insert also fashioned a basketweave sheath for the piece.
(SharpByCoop image)

KIRBY LAMBERT
Japanese letters spell out the maker's name and date. The alder scabbard was made for a W2 sushi knife with a bog oak handle.
(SharpByCoop image)

MATT GREGORY
Based on Mike Walton's design and inspired by Bob Lum's work, the tanto showcases a CPM-154 blade, an African blackwood handle, and a Jill Gregory leather sheath.
(SharpByCoop image)

» EDDIE STALCUP

Stingray skin stitched within the leather sheath adds flavor to an already tasty 9-inch CTS-XHP hunter with a raised false edge and dyed black ash burl handle.

« DAVID LISCH

For a damascus fixed-blade hunter in a mammoth ivory handle, a Francesca Ritchie Wilburn leather sheath completes the package.
(SharpByCoop image)

» JOHN COHEA

The frontier bowie showcases a Chad Nichols damascus blade, walrus ivory handle, wrought iron guard and a tanned, carved, fringed and beaded leather sheath.
(SharpByCoop image)

» ANDREAS KALANI

A high-carbon damascus, ironwood-handle knife that combines influences of a Japanese tanto, Nepalese kukri and American bowie deserves a carved and inlaid leather belt sheath.
(SharpByCoop image)

Colossally Carved

erhaps it started with a bit of whittling on the front porch, talking to the neighbors and turning a piece of birch into a human stick figure, but these are no whittlers. The ones carving knife handles and spacers are adept at the art of sculpting semi-pliable material. The skill level is a bit above par, so to speak.

One carver told me it was more about the material speaking to him. When pressed further, he said it is not so much taking away material but instead leaving what is supposed to be there. When I asked him how he knew what to leave untouched, he said, "it reveals itself within the grains and grooves." Now that is an artist.

And the eyes do not lie, his or ours. Gaze at the knives on this and the following pages, and one sees some colossally carved pieces with sexy, sinister, sleek and sumptuous figures emerging from media. They revealed themselves, alright, with the artisan knifemakers taking full advantage and carving the pieces until masterpieces emerge.

JON CHRISTENSEN
A themed fixed dagger, the "Garden Walk" showcases a "Rose Garden" mosaic damascus blade and a carved fossil walrus ivory handle. The frame is wrought iron with bronze liners and pins. *(SharpByCoop image)*

PAR-OLOF EKLUND
A Sami-style half-horn hunter employs a twist-pattern Damasteel blade and an engraved and carved reindeer antler handle with stabilized sallow root spacers. *(BladeGallery.com image)*

RICK DUNKERLEY
The impressive piece features gold inlay, file work, carving, stippling and, of course, the hand forging of the damascus blade and bolsters. *(Eric Eggly, PointSeven image)*

FRED OTT
A fighter enters the ring in a clay-zone-heated W2 carbon steel blade, an antiqued bronze guard and a carved, spalted tamarind handle with ebony and ironwood spacers. *(BladeGallery.com image)*

RICHARD DAWES
The African blackwood handles on a pair of Bill Bagwell style A2 bird's-head bowies are carved to represent Huginn and Muninn, two mythical ravens that attend Odin. *(SharpByCoop image)*

STEVE MYERS
There's as much character in the carved sambar stag handle as there is in that 1095-and-15N20 damascus blade. *(Caleb Royer image)*

➤ MARK BANFIELD
The 19.5-inch recurved fighter enters the fray in a hand-forged 1075 blade with hamon (temper line), sculpted nickel silver fittings, and hand-carved African blackwood and moose antler handle, the latter in a Celtic knot pattern.
(BladeGallery.com image)

⌃ JOE EDSON
A Yu-Shoku blade of carbon steel set between layers of stainless, brass, and copper pivots out from a "brain coral" carbon fiber handle carved into dragon scales.
(BladeGallery.com image)

⌃ PAUL DISTEFANO
The sleek, sexy bowie boasts a 13-inch mosaic damascus blade, a giant, sweeping S-guard and a carved wooly mammoth ivory handle in a floral Sakura/cherry blossoms motif. *(Caleb Royer image)*

« CHUCK SCHUETTE
A mosaic damascus hunter gets the full handle treatment—bas relief carving and texturing in mastodon ivory—capped off by a stippled pommel.
(SharpByCoop image)

« HARLAN "SID" SUEDMEIER
The eagle head pommel bowie is alive and well thanks to some Troy Lampkins carving of the walrus tusk handle on a damascus beauty.
(SharpByCoop image)

Show Us
Your Dimples

Come on, show us those dimples, and maybe the pearly grips, too. It is such a simple thing—like a handsome dude with endearing dimples—to carve, peen or otherwise hammer the bolsters, handles or even blades of fixed knives and folders for added aesthetic appeal.

Some would say dimpling also gives finger guards added purchase, but the "added purchase" part is hopefully reserved for the extra couple bucks a maker might get for paying attention to such details as peening the bolsters.

It is all about the details. The collectors know it, and the makers understand wholeheartedly about every last detail being perfect, with no gaps where the dimpled guards and bolsters meet handle material, no wiggling of the blade, rattling of the knife when shaken.

It is just another feather in the makers' caps, more ammunition in the arsenal, further proof in the pudding that the craftsmen making modern knives are skilled and self-aware, showing us their abilities, creativity, style and, well, dimples.

《 BUBBA CROUCH
No detail was left untouched on the Panama-style trapper, not the herringbone damascus blade, bark mammoth ivory handle or dimpled (beaten and blued) copper bolsters.
(SharpByCoop image)

» JAMES HUSE II
Dimpling on either end of the mammoth tooth handle adds flavor to the long fighter with a top front edge. *(Eric Eggly, PointSeven image)*

« BENJAMIN KAMON
A stainless Gyuto chef's knife is done up in a san mai blade with a 1.2519 steel core, a "denty" exterior, as the maker says, titanium bolster and ringed Gidgee wood handle.
(SharpByCoop image)

« EDDIE STALCUP
With brain coral handle scales and dimpled stainless bolsters, the file-worked CPM-154 hunter is the most handsome in the forest.

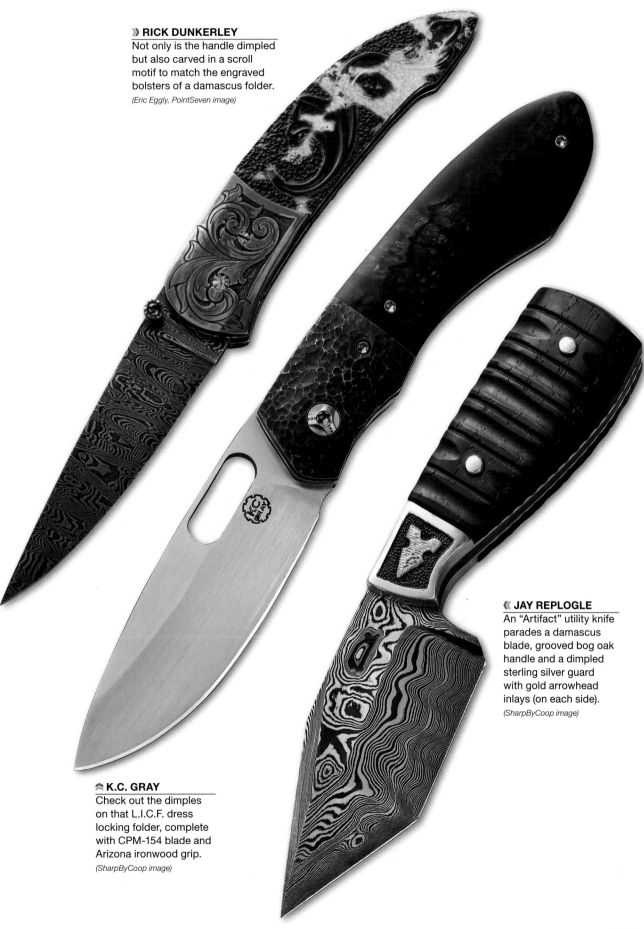

» RICK DUNKERLEY
Not only is the handle dimpled but also carved in a scroll motif to match the engraved bolsters of a damascus folder.

(Eric Eggly, PointSeven image)

« JAY REPLOGLE
An "Artifact" utility knife parades a damascus blade, grooved bog oak handle and a dimpled sterling silver guard with gold arrowhead inlays (on each side).

(SharpByCoop image)

⌃ K.C. GRAY
Check out the dimples on that L.I.C.F. dress locking folder, complete with CPM-154 blade and Arizona ironwood grip.

(SharpByCoop image)

Controlled Damascus Chaos

» SHAYNE CARTER
Tightly patterned Turkish twist "W's" damascus pulls cutting duty on a mammoth ivory-handle hunter. *(SharpByCoop image)*

» IAN ROGERS
Including mammoth tooth accents and an Arizona desert ironwood handle, the Gyuto chef's knife comes in a raindrop-pattern Niolox and AEB-L stainless damascus blade. *(BladeGallery.com image)*

» JOSHUA PRINCE
An integral damascus "Laniakea" model is beautifully etched and includes a decomposed, stabilized and spalted white oak handle. *(SharpByCoop image)*

» BILL POOR
With feather and static-like patterns, the controlled damascus chaos comes in hunting knife form handled traditionally in burl. *(Eric Eggly, PointSeven image)*

» WESS BARNHILL
The feather damascus blade of a mammoth ivory-handle bowie is easy on the eyes. *(SharpByCoop image)*

» ANDREW MEERS
It is as if flames are licking both edges of the hand-forged, multi-bar damascus dagger blade, accompanied by a carved ebony handle and a Parkerized mild steel ferrule with fine silver engraved lily pads. *(BladeGallery.com image)*

» MATTHEW BERRY
A "Trondheim Berserker" Viking sword features a carved caribou antler handle, a cast bronze guard and pommel, and a damascus blade forged with a serpent core of high carbon cable steel surrounded by 15N20 and 1075 laminate bars. *(SharpByCoop image)*

» DAVID TUTHILL
A San Francisco treat, the blade of this cocobolo-handle chef's knife is forged from a suspension cable of the Golden Gate Bridge. *(BladeGallery.com image)*

≪ PAT BIGGIN

Inspired by an early 1900's butcher knife, the five-bar damascus piece with salt-blued guard and ringed Gidgee wood handle has character and depth. *(Cory Martin Imaging)*

≪ WILLIAM BRIGHAM

One upstages the other—the patterning of the feather damascus blade and that of the amboyna burl and sapwood handle. *(SharpByCoop image)*

≪ SAM EDDLEMAN

Considering the Bertie Rietveld "Dragonskin" damascus, the nylon-wrapped purple stingray skin handle was an appropriate choice for the tanto. *(BladeGallery.com image)*

≪ RUDY DEAN

The twist damascus head and curly English walnut haft of the pipe tomahawk go together like buckskins and moccasins. *(SharpByCoop image)*

≪ RYU LIM

The random pattern damascus camp knife parades a pinecone handle. *(SharpByCoop image)*

≪ CHARLIE ELLIS

When you forge an S-ground "fudge ripple" damascus blade for a chef's knife and combine it with a hand-contoured charcoal G-Carta handle, you're cooking with Crisco. *(BladeGallery.com image)*

≪ BRANDON HAMPTON

Digitized readouts run across the 3V and 154CM damascus blade of a Western chef's knife in a stabilized pink burl handle. *(SharpByCoop image)*

≪ MAX BUCCI

His uncle's idea, the damascus "Mezzaluna" (lowrider), features ebony handles with silver/copper Mokume-gane rings. An "S"-grind runs down the blade to expose the smooth damascus. *(Caleb Royer image)*

BILL BURKE

A "River of Fire" flows across the blade of a Gyoto Japanese chef's knife handled in African blackwood. *(Eric Eggly, PointSeven image)*

JASON KRAUS and LUKE DELLMYER

Former competitors on Discovery Channel's "Master of Arms" and now friends, Dellmyer provided the feather damascus, and Krause Forge finished it, adding a stabilized maple burl handle. *(SharpByCoop image)*

MARDI MESHEJIAN

Patterns within the hand-forged 1080 and 15N20 blade of a chef's knife are parallel and unparalleled, complemented by a Shibuichi bolster, a marbled carbon fiber handle and a quilted maple frame. *(BladeGallery.com image)*

BRETT NOAKE

The "flamethrower" damascus blade is as hot as the mammoth tooth handle on the maker's "Uncle Mike" skinner. *(SharpByCoop image)*

ANDREA LISCH

Feather damascus and spalted maple provide the one-two punch for a 14 1/8-inch chef's knife. *(Eric Eggly, PointSeven image)*

KEVIN CASEY

The maker's feather damascus follows the lines of the bowie blade, guarded via wrought iron and anchored by a fossil walrus ivory handle. *(SharpByCoop image)*

VAN BARNETT

The "Vader Flipper" combines a gun-blued damascus blade with a stacked handle of blued O1 carbon steel and bronze riveting. *(BladeGallery.com image)*

GABE MABRY

An integral chef's knife showcases a walrus ivory handle, and a gorgeous Steve Grosvenor damascus blade made up of 80CrV2, 52100, CruforgeV and 15N20 steels. *(SharpByCoop image)*

JOSH FISHER

While the 15N20-and-1084 damascus dazzles, the curly Tasmanian blackwood handle holds its own. *(Caleb Royer image)*

« VLADIMIR KOLENKO
Bertie Rietveld's "Nebula" damascus blade gets top billing on an art dagger that also showcases a mammoth ivory handle embellished with sterling silver, 14-karat gold, garnets and lapis lazuli. *(SharpByCoop image)*

« DAVID MCCONNELL
It might just be damascus and faux ivory to some, but to others, the knife is a study in design, flow, movement and pattern. *(Cory Martin Imaging)*

« BRIAN SELLERS
The modified ladder-pattern damascus blade is oh-so-sweet on a stag-handle sub-hilt fighter. (*SharpByCoop image)*

« JAMIE LUNDELL and MATTHEW BERRY
A prime example of a Roman gladius sword, Lundell forged and etched the 1080-and-15N20 damascus blade. At the same time, Berry fashioned the buffalo horn, silver and bronze hilt adorned with rubies. *(SharpByCoop image)*

« KAJ EMBRETSEN
A bolt of lightning strikes across the three-bar damascus blade of a back-lock folder handled in sambar stag. *(BladeGallery.com image)*

« BILL BURKE
Dragon's breath damascus throws flames across the blade of a yanagi-ba-bocho sashimi knife anchored by a red morrell (eucalyptus) wood and musk ox horn handle with a gold spacer. *(Eric Eggly, PointSeven image)*

« SCOTT JORAM SWEDER
The bowie blade is a multi-bar affair including "Gordidian knot," ladder and mosaic twist damascus patterns combined with a mild steel guard, red mallee burl handle and an antler spacer. *(Caleb Royer image)*

« ANDREW BURKE
A bold Turkish twist damascus pattern defines the blade and bolsters of a mammoth ivory-handle locking-liner folder. *(BladeGallery.com image)*

« CHARLIE MAJORS
Like a good feather damascus pattern does, the lines splay out on the blade of an engraved fixed blade with a tapered tang. *(Eric Eggly, PointSeven image)*

ERIK MCCRIGHT
Occasionally, the random patterns play out perfectly, here in a blade handled with stag. *(Caleb Royer image)*

JOHN M. COHEA
The copper wash of a random-damascus blade matches the wrought iron bolster of one fine fossil walrus ivory-handle bowie. *(SharpByCoop image)*

DAVID LISCH
This showstopper starts with a fossilized walrus ivory handle and ends with multiple damascus guard and blade patterns, including a dragon-tooth edge. *(Eric Eggly, PointSeven image)*

KEVIN HARVEY
A Nordic hunter is the beneficiary of an African wattle burl handle and guard and a raindrops and ladder "W's"-pattern damascus blade.
(BladeGallery.com image)

KYLE ROYER
The fine feather damascus blade of the "Mamute Hunter" is accompanied by a fossil mammoth ivory handle and 24k-gold inlays. *(Caleb Royer image)*

JURGEN SCHANZ
A flipper folder wears its stainless damascus patterning like a cheetah wears its spots, its sculpted body moving in rhythm. *(BladeGallery.com image)*

JOHN H. DAVIS
No mere stag-handle bowie, "firestorm" damascus enters the fray, as does ivy-pattern file work on the blade spine and a clamshell finger guard.
(SharpByCoop image)

JEFF DAVIDSON
With a chain damascus blade, the wood-handle fixed blade will fly off the shelf. *(Eric Eggly, PointSeven image)*

CHARLES CARPENTER
"Texas Wind" damascus meets up with a damascus guard, copper spacer and desert ironwood handle.
(Caleb Royer image)

HALEY DESROSIERS
Somehow, the name "Batsauce" damascus just fits the blade patterning on an integral bird-and-trout knife with a Hawaiian Koa handle. Francesca Wilburn-Ritchie fashioned a caiman-tail leather sheath for the piece. *(SharpByCoop image)*

RICK DUNKERLEY
The pattern spans from bolster to blade, with gold highlights and sculpted lines to complement the carved handle. *(Eric Eggly, PointSeven image)*

MIKE TYRE
The blade, guard, bolsters and frame of a Western cowboy bowie are forged from the same feather damascus billet, with only sambar stag breaking up the party. *(SharpByCoop image)*

JOSEPH SCHRUM
The Gyuto model gets the royal 1095-and-15N20 damascus blade treatment, along with an ancient redgum handle and fossil mammoth ivory spacer. *(Caleb Royer image)*

PETER PRUYN
Few are the pipe axes with twist damascus heads, filtered bowls and draught holes through ash handles. *(SharpByCoop image)*

DALE MILLER
Imagine the satisfaction after etching the hand-forged W's-damascus blade of the African blackwood-handle chef's knife to bring out the pattern. *(BladeGallery.com image)*

SCOTT GALLAGHER
Shockwaves were felt across the blade of a fossil walrus ivory-handle bowie with 24k-gold inlays. *(SharpByCoop image)*

PEYTON RAMM
Ribbon damascus wends its way down the blade of a locking-liner folder, complete with giraffe bone handle. *(Caleb Royer image)*

ZACK JONAS
Follow the "river of fire" damascus pattern from its blade tip down to the black G-10 bolster and dyed birch handle of a Kiritsuke model. *(SharpByCoop image)*

⟫ JACKSON RUMBLE
The dazzling 1075-and-15N20 damascus blade is forged with an integral guard and given a desert ironwood handle to hold onto. *(Caleb Royer image)*

⟫ PETER MARTIN
Who knew bubble damascus blades would be a thing, appropriately executed here on a pearl-handled flipper folder with dimpled titanium pocket clip? *(Cory Martin Imaging)*

⟫ JOHN PHILLIPS
Welcome the Santoku chef's knife in stainless Damasteel, synthetic horn and cottonwood burl. *(SharpByCoop image)*

⟫ BRENT STUBBLEFIELD
Inspired by a kukri, the multi-bar twist-damascus blade is anchored by a wrought iron guard, hippo tusk spacer and African blackwood handle.

(Caleb Royer image)

⟫ DAVID S. KULIS
"Dragonskin" damascus by Bertie Rietveld is used to full effect for the blade of a flipper folder, matched up with a Vegas Forge Dragonskin Damtanium handle and brightly anodized bolsters.

(SharpByCoop image)

⟫ TOBIN HILL
Check out the slim "River of Fire" damascus blade on a bird-and-trout slip-joint folder with mahogany jigged bone handle. *(BladeGallery.com image)*

⟫ RANDY HAAS
A bold bird's-eye-pattern damascus blade takes center stage on a fossil walrus tusk-handle chef's knife with a mosaic damascus bolster.

(SharpByCoop image)

⟫ JORDON BERTHELOT
A sculpted leaf-shaped HHH Star Feather damascus blade is married up with a carbon fiber guard and maple handle. *(Caleb Royer image)*

⟫ MATT PARKINSON
A damascus chef's knife parades a G-10 spacer and stabilized birch handle.

(SharpByCoop image)

« C. LUIS PINA
The damascus blade of a curly mango-handle bread knife is hand forged to shape from 1080 and 15N20 carbon steels. *(BladeGallery.com image)*

« CARL COLSON
A Vineland-pattern Damasteel blade dresses up a fixed blade semi-skinner in a rosewood burl handle. *(SharpByCoop image)*

« CHAD KENNEDY
Of sole authorship, the chef's knife is almost unrecognizable as such, looking like an art piece in a serpentine feather damascus blade, integral guard and a silver wire-inlaid maple handle. *(Caleb Royer image)*

« MATT ROBERTS
The blade is forged from an industrial crane cable and affixed to a stainless guard and a figured ash handle. *(SharpByCoop image)*

« CORRIE SCHOEMAN
The raindrop damascus blade pattern gives the bone-handle folder movement. *(BladeGallery. com image)*

« CHRIS SHARP
While ribbons of damascus flit across the blade, a hot-blued guard and pommel and spalted maple handle hold their own. *(SharpByCoop image)*

« CHRIS DREW
The Chad Nichols "Meadows" damascus blade sets the mood, matched up nicely with an ironwood burl handle and mosaic pins. *(Caleb Royer image)*

« AARON WILBURN
A mammoth ivory-handle bowie sports a handsome 1084-and-15N20 damascus blade. *(SharpByCoop image)*

« IAN PICKARSK
The Mike Norris damascus blade of the dress tactical folder is a nice contrast to the zirconium bolsters and titanium handle and frame. *(SharpByCoop image)*

Sculptors of Steel

If you do not allow limitations, then there are none. No one apparently told the knifemakers that sculpting steel is akin to slicing diamonds, chipping through bulletproof glass or puncturing titanium, but it would not have stopped them anyway.

One does have to wonder if choosing steel as a sculpting medium makes a person masochistic or at the very least prone to punishment. All joking aside, how knifemakers manipulate and form metal into attractive shapes and designs is remarkable, and collectors and enthusiasts are the beneficiaries of their artistic slants.

Working in the world of knives, these sculptors of steel are visionaries whose imaginations come to life in the form of blades, bolsters, guards and grips. They form steel and other metallic alloys into aesthetically superior edged tools, each meant to be used and admired. They are as easy in the mitts as they are on the eyes.

Thus is the goal of makers of fine blades in the first place—to create beautifully utilitarian works of art. They are the sculptors of steel, and they are not nearly as masochistic or misguided as one might think. The proof is in the pudding.

« JAMIE LUNDELL
As curvaceous as a dragon's tail, the sword sports a 1080-and-15N20 damascus blade, leather-wrapped wood hilt and a bronze guard and dragonhead pommel, the latter with sapphire eyes.
(SharpByCoop image)

⌄ TOM STERLING
With a 1084 blade sculpted as if it was flint knapped, the push dagger also parades an engraved tellurium copper handle and 24k-gold accents.

(BladeGallery.com image)

« DAVID BROADWELL
Sharing his vision for an Art Deco "Egyptian Revival" dagger, the maker outfitted it with a David Lisch mosaic damascus blade and set Ray Cover to work engraving, inlaying and sculpting the piece in platinum, copper, rose gold, yellow gold and zirconium.

(SharpByCoop image)

« DON FOGG
If you can make a dagger blade look like that—as if shards of metal formed a matrix in the steel's core and on the collar and pommel, then you've reached enlightenment.

⌃ MICHAEL ZIEBA
With a san mai blade forged by Chad Nichols in "Boomerang" damascus with a CTS-XHP steel core, the art dagger reaches "Enlightenment" via its sculpted solid silver, gold, bronze, copper and nickel handle, not to mention a frame inlaid with diamonds and a tourmaline gemstone.

(SharpByCoop image)

» MAX BERGER
"War Wounds" began life as a 130-pound billet of 440C stainless steel and ended in its current 37.5-ounce dragon-like form with a bit of help from its maker.

» MATTHEW BERRY
With a damascus blade forged by Nick Anger, the "Gynomorphic Sword" has female physical characteristics, alright, sculpted in bronze.
(SharpByCoop image)

» HIDETOSHI NAKAYAMA
The one-of-a-kind D2 slip-joint folder showcases a SUS304 stainless handle sculpted into wolf jaw form.
(BladeGallery.com image)

» CORY MARTIN
Between the "beach front" san mai damascus blade and hand-carved titanium handle with a vent hole so the pattern welded steel shows when closed, the frame-lock flipper folder is a captivating creature.
(Cory Martin Imaging)

San Mai Samurai

If it were not such a gorgeous way of forging blades, this chapter would be in the "Trends" section of the book, but my gosh, it deserves a "State of the Art" classification.

San mai blades, those forged from multiple steels with hardened inner cores, and thus, edges, sandwiched between damascus or softer steel outer layers, truly have taken over the handmade knife industry.

It may or might not be a trend, but perhaps a revolution. And, yes, the blades are revolutionary. While not new, the art of forging san mai blades has exploded in the last decade and a half, and makers have the right to be proud. After etching a properly forged san mai blade, the aesthetic properties are incredible.

With the blades having hard edges and softer outer cores, the utilitarian purposes are just as noteworthy. San mai blades are the definition of practical art. Their makers are the san mai samurai of the knife industry, cutting down the competition in single swipes.

》 PAT BIGGIN
Like a vein of gold in rock, the copper san mai damascus is a sight for sore eyes anchored by a mahogany handle and elk antler spacer. *(Cory Martin Imaging)*

《 WILL MANNING

With a san mai blade forged from bourbon barrel straps, including a 52100 core, the handle is spalted Georgia red oak with an African blackwood bolster. (*Caleb Royer image*)

》 DAN KEFFELER and SAM TAYLOR

After research, the makers think this is the first heat-treatable san mai titanium katana, complete with a cord-wrapped Terro-Tuff and carbon fiber hilt.

(SharpByCoop image)

⌃ BILL BURKE

The san mai blade is as sweet at the box elder burl and carbon fiber handle. (*Eric Eggly, PointSeven image*)

» CLAUDIO and ARIEL SOBRAL (CAS Brothers)
The Viper strikes via a hand-forged san mai blade with a 1095 carbon steel core and 420 stainless steel sides, its contoured desert ironwood body writhing. *(BladeGallery.com image)*

« CURT ZIMMERMANN
The appealing patterns of san mai blades keep piling up. This one is a fighter in ball-bearing steel and a fossilized walrus ivory handle.
(SharpByCoop image)

« BURT FOSTER and MATTHEW GREGORY
Burt forged an 80CrV2 and 410 stainless san mai blade for the Presentation Tanto, while Matthew outfitted the piece with a cord-wrapped carbon fiber handle.
(SharpByCoop image))

« HERUCUS BLOMERUS
The singular san mai flipper folder showcases Vinland-pattern Damasteel bolsters and lightning strike carbon fiber handle scales.
(BladeGallery.com image))

» JOHN ARNOLD
Silver strike carbon fiber handle scales and zirconium bolsters are nice accouterments to the Damacore san mai blade forged by Damasteel.
(BladeGallery.com image)

» CURTIS HAALAND
It is an "Apocalyptic Fighter," alright, donning a wicked 410 stainless and 80CrV2 san mai blade, a wrought iron guard, and a black stabilized mango handle.
(SharpByCoop image)

» PETER MARTIN
The san mai here is a "Quicksilver" damascus blade complemented by zirconium bolsters and a Timascus handle and back bar. *(Cory Martin Imaging)*

⌃ TYLER HACKBARTH
The "Go Mai" blade is a 50-layer damascus with a W2 core accompanied by a 7,500-year-old bog oak handle and a yellow cedar bolster.
(Caleb Royer image

≪ JEREMY BARTLETT
Five inches of san mai blade steel help define a drop point hunter in a stag handle. *(Eric Eggly, PointSeven image)*

≪ ANDRE THORBURN
A san mai blade, engraved and differentially anodized titanium bolsters, and a red/black carbon-fiber handle populate a flipper folder.
(BladeGallery.com image)

≪ DAN TOMPKINS
The 52100-and-copper san mai blade of the 9-inch Gyuto is from Dion Damascus and married here to a dyed box elder burl grip.
(Caleb Royer image)

⌃ TOM BUCKNER
The stripes of the chef's knife extend from the SG2 and damascus san mai blade onto the black and white ebony handle and then to the matching wooden saya (sheath).
(SharpByCoop image)

» **K.C. GRAY**
A "Large Squeegee" model showcases a Vegas Forge san mai damascus blade, cross-cut mammoth ivory handle scales and Timascus bolsters.

(SharpByCoop image)

⌄ **JORDON BERTHELOT**
A mini tanto sports a Justin Reynolds tri-stack damascus blade over an O1 core and a Honduran rosewood handle.

(Caleb Royer image)

» **JAMES KALKBRENNER**
San mai damascus has come so far, it vies for attention with woolly mammoth tusk scales.

(Caleb Royer image)

« **MARDI MESHEJIAN**
San mai, my, my … the hand-forged chef's knife with Shibuichi (silver and copper) bolster and octagonal stabilized sycamore handle has one gorgeous blade.

(BladeGallery.com image)

BRAD MILLMAN
The "Wolftooth" bowie boasts a 1095-and-15N20 damascus blade with a 1084 core, a curly Tasmanian blackwood handle and a forged copper guard. *(Caleb Royer image)*

STEVE RANDALL
The smart san mai bowie blade is accompanied by a dyed sambar stag handle, stainless steel guard and blued fittings.
(SharpByCoop image)

JACKSON RUMBLE
The san mai blade of a Santoku chef's knife features a 52100 carbon-steel core sandwiched by satin-finished 416 stainless outer layers, accompanied by an octagonal 7,500-year-old ancient red gum handle.
(BladeGallery.com image)

JUSTIN BURTON
A twist on a seax knife, the blade is of "Go-Mai" construction with a random-pattern damascus outer jacket and a 15N20 and 1084 core. The handle material is curly maple.
(Caleb Royer image)

« CORRIE SCHOEMAN
Showcasing a black G-10 handle with lightning strike carbon fiber overlays and running on caged bearings, the action of the san mai folder is exceptional. *(BladeGallery.com image)*

» JAMES OATLEY
The Yu-Shoku san mai blade of the Gyuto chef's knife combines a V-Toku2 carbon steel core with Mokumé gane sides, accompanied by a dyed and stabilized maple burl handle.
(BladeGallery.com image)

« JOSH WHITE
The 180-layer blade is damascus clad over a 1095 core and accompanied by a dyed, stabilized and checkered maple burl grip and a G-10 guard and inlays.
(SharpByCoop image)

« WENDON SHARMAN
The dogtooth pattern of the san mai blade gives the sambar-stag-handle fighter some bite. *(Caleb Royer image)*

FACTORY TRENDS

Nowhere is cutting-edge technology more apparent than in the production knife arena. Not only have knife manufacturers seen an influx of competition within the United States and from every corner of the world, but also rapid increases in blade patterns, styles, mechanisms, gadgets, sheaths, materials and steels have upped the ante on factory edges.

For millennia, knife manufacturers looked within to their own designers and engineers for new patterns to produce. In the wake of the custom knife renaissance that occurred in the 1960s and '70s, production knife companies were forced to look outside of their walls and collaborate with those fashioning handmade knives.

At first, the machining and tooling wasn't up to par, and production companies struggled to emulate handmade knife patterns, materials, steels and mechanical wizardry. It took an overhaul of manufacturing equipment across the board to meet the advancements in technology, steels and materials.

Welcome to 2021/'22, a time when quality is inherent to factory knives, handmade pieces and mid-tech lines. Whether buying online, at shows or from area stores, knife users and enthusiasts have more choices and price levels than ever before.

Factory companies, with the help of custom makers, designers and engineers with whom they collaborate, are once again leading the way in innovation and technology, but they probably shouldn't get too comfortable.

HOW TO SHARPEN SUPER STEELS

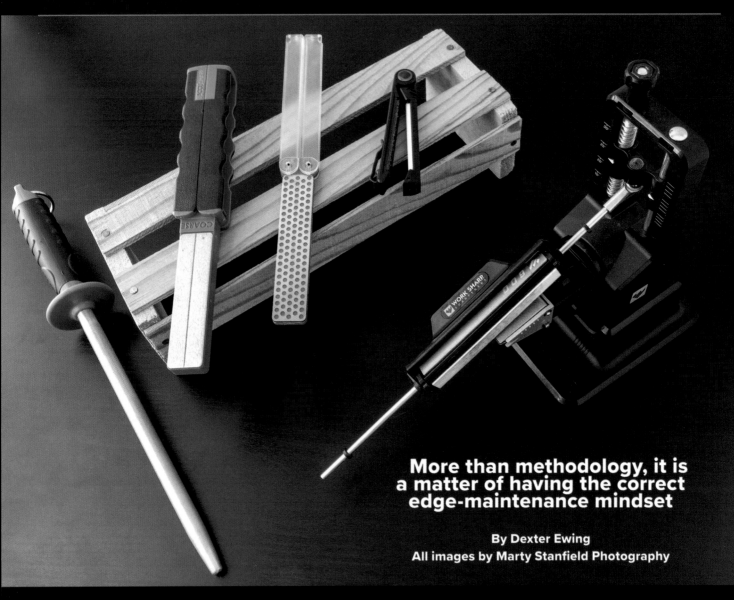

More than methodology, it is a matter of having the correct edge-maintenance mindset

By Dexter Ewing
All images by Marty Stanfield Photography

I f you are like me, you love to experience the latest and greatest in knife technology and materials. Blade steels are without a doubt at the center of this fascination.

The steels employed on today's high-end factory and custom knives push the envelope in terms of wear resistance. They outpace traditional high-carbon steels with the ability to power through a variety of tough materials, as well as perform such chores as field dressing animals, and with minimal maintenance necessary between edge honing.

Proper sharpening sessions are fewer and far between with super steels. A common complaint, regardless of preferred alloy, however, is that super steels are difficult to sharpen, a result of their extreme wear resistance properties. The ability of the

The sharpeners featured in this story are, from left to right, the Lansky Diamond Sharp Stick, AccuSharp Diamond Paddle, DMT Double-Sided Diafold, Benchmade Edge Maintenance Tool and the Work Sharp Precision Adjust Sharpener.

The AccuSharp Diamond Paddle folding sharpener features a double-sided honing surface with coarse and fine grits to make fast work of restoring an edge. The handle halves fold over the sharpener to protect the surfaces while in a bag, toolchest or glove box.

steels to go the distance when it counts is the same characteristic that works against knife users when it comes to blade maintenance.

In this article, we will discuss how to properly keep your blades in tip-top sharp shape, ready for action and without a significant investment of time and effort.

First, let us define what we mean by "super steels." Stainless super steels are manufactured using particle metallurgy technology, meaning they begin life as tiny particles that are heated and formed into more homogenous structures. There is more even distribution of carbides in the steels as well, which enhances cutting performance and edge holding. In general, particle metallurgy steels rank high in dimensional stability, toughness and grindability compared with other steels that are manufactured via conventional melting processes (how lesser grades of steel are made).

If you are familiar with high-end factory and custom knives, I am sure that you are certainly no stranger to steels such as Crucible Industries' CPM S30V, CPM S35VN, CPM S45VN, CPM 154 and CPM 20CV; Carpenter Technology's CTS 204P and CTS XHP; and Bohler's M390 MICROCLEAN and ELMAX SuperClean.

Again, they are all particle metallurgy steels, specially manufactured to provide a long-wearing blade for various applications, from tactical to hunting, and anything in between.

Why are super steels so difficult to resharpen? Simply put, the engineered characteristics of particle metallurgy steels that make them incredibly wear resistant also make them difficult to hone. When you sharpen a blade, you are wearing away the steel in tiny amounts.

From Dull to Sharp

If you take a knife made with one of

the 400 series stainless steels (420HC, 420J2, 440A, and to some extent, 440C), you can use the blade until it goes completely dull, meaning it will not cut anymore when you push it through food or other media. You can then resharpen the blade and get it working again with a sharp edge.

Try doing the same thing with any particle metallurgy steel, and your results will not be the same. All I can say is good luck!

Taking CPM S30V to completely dull then trying to resharpen on a manual sharpener such as a Lansky, you will be spending a considerable amount of time getting the edge geometry correct again. It is why folks dislike particle metallurgy steels; they cannot resharpen them. It is nearly impossible outside of using a method with variable-speed, motorized abrasive belts. Most knife enthusiast do not own such equipment, but instead possess manual sharpeners.

If you like the concept of long-lasting particle metallurgy steel but hate to maintain it because of the significant investment of time it takes to work on a dull blade, I have some important tips for you! Despair no more; it is a matter of changing one's approach and thinking.

Typically, folks take a blade down to being dull before they attempt to resharpen. With particle metallurgy super steels, you must switch from an "edge sharpening" mindset to an "edge maintenance" way of thinking. With the latter, you really do not take the cutting edge down to completely dull before you begin to work on it. Depending on the frequency of use, you will be maintaining the edge several times a week or possibly daily or twice daily. Again, the frequency depends on

The Edge Maintenance Tool from Benchmade is made by Work Sharp and incorporates a fine grit ceramic rod and a leather strip for quick touch ups. The entire sharpener folds to a compact size and includes a pocket clip much like many Benchmade folders.

The DMT Double-Sided Diafold features two grits—coarse and fine—in one easy-to-use sharpener for the ultimate in convenience. For minor touch ups, the fine grit should suffice.

how much you use your knife.

Think of the profile of the edge bevel. It is basically a "V" shape that results after a proper sharpening at the factory before the knife is shipped to a customer. As you use the knife, the point of the "V" gradually flattens. Regardless of the level of steel, all blade steels wear like this, but the grade determines how slow the wear occurs. The higher grades of steel, being more wear resistant than non-powder metallurgical alloys, hold an edge longer.

So, when the point of the "V" becomes flat, that is when we think "Uh oh, it is time to resharpen" and attempt to give the "V" shape a point again by using whatever sharpener that we favor. Trying to reconstruct this point is what will take longer with particle metallurgy steels.

Contrarily the "edge maintenance" mindset attempts to keep and hold a freshly sharpened edge and "V" profile. As a blade is used, the point begins to flatten and before that flat part becomes clearly defined, it is taken to the sharpener for an edge touchup, bringing the crisp point of the double-sided bevel back to the "V" configuration. Therefore, the knife user always has a keen, properly constructed edge geometry on the blade.

Minimal Force Applied

When the edge loses its ability to cut with minimal force applied, this is a perfect indication that it is time to hone the edge and bring it back to hair-popping sharpness. It is that simple. The knife user addresses the blade in more frequent intervals than he or she would with a full resharpening routine.

Now that we have covered the proper technique to approach in maintaining super steels, the next question is, "What sharpener do I use?" Regardless of what system you choose, I feel that diamond sharpeners provide the best results on super steels, given their aggressive nature to abrade away material, and they last a long time as well, with minimal upkeep required. Ceramic hones also work well, though they are not my first choice. Please stay away from sharpeners that require you to pull the blade through a slot. Such hones remove a

bit too much metal on the blade, causing damage and altering the edge profile in the long run.

Should your only option be a pull-through sharpener, use it sparing- ly with light pressure. Even with such caution, they ruin blades in time and should be avoided for expensive, high-end factory and custom knives.

Here are some recom- mendations for sharpeners that I have used on knives with super steel blades and that have worked well for me. I am sure that you will experience similar results.

DMT's Diafold line of sharpeners features a convenient fold-up design that incorporates handle halves to encapsulate a 5-inch-long hone and protect its surface during transport and storage. As its name suggests, the FWCX Coarse/Extra Coarse Double-Sided Diafold sharpener includes Extra Coarse and Coarse grit diamond sharpening surfaces, with the company's trademark DMT polka-dot appearance. The hones are easy to carry and use for sharpening on the go or at home. The manufacturer's suggested retail price (MSRP) is $49.29, which makes it a worthwhile investment considering the types of knives that you can effectively sharpen on this one.

The GATCO Tri-Seps Diamond sharpening stick is available in ceramic and diamond varieties, giving you a choice of honing elements. The triangular profile of the sharpener allows it to address plain edge blades on the flats and serrations on the pointed corners. Measuring 4 ½ inches long, the Tri- Seps incorporates rubber endcaps with angle guides for ease of use

The Diamond Sharp Stick from Lansky is a hand-held diamond-coated rod measuring 9 inches in length and suitable for fixed blades as well as folding knives of all sizes. The ergonomic handle features a dual-molded grip and integral guard for safety.

The Work Sharp Precision Adjust Sharpener is an angle guide sharpening kit that helps to maintain the desired honing angle, taking all guesswork out of the task.

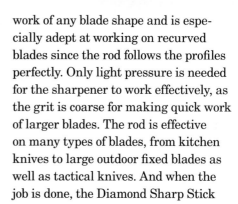

and to protect the sharpener. The ceramic Tri-Seps retails for $11.25, and the diamond Tri-Seps carries an MSRP of $23.99. Each includes a ball chain loop to fasten the sharpener to a backpack strap or any other convenient loop that will allow it to be close at hand when needed.

AccuSharp's Diamond Paddle Sharpener offers two honing grits in one package. The coarse and fine diamond grits each encompass about 3 ½ inches of sharpening surface. Like the DMT Diafold, the handles of the AccuSharp Diamond Paddle Sharpener fold up to encase the hone and provide protection for the sharpening surfaces when not in use. The handles have textured rubber grips, making them easier to hold. The MSRP is $28.99.

Work Sharp's Precision Adjust sharpener incorporates a clamp for securing a blade to the frame of the hone, and an adjustable angle guide rod. The guide rod is attached to a unique three-sided hone that features coarse- and fine-grit diamond, and fine-grit ceramic sharpening surfaces. The hone rotates and locks into place, allowing you to select one of the sharpening surfaces.

Angle Adjustment

This is a much better alternative to having three separate hones to manipulate. The angle of the guide rod is adjustable via a knob at the top. Turning the knob clockwise increases the angle and turning it counterclockwise lowers the angle. The exact angle settings are clearly marked on the uprights of the sharpener.

The guide rod is also affixed to its carrier, as opposed to the hone itself as with other similar systems. Because the unit controls the angle, this eliminates the guesswork of maintaining the proper edge bevel. The Work Sharp makes edge maintenance easy and carries an MSRP of $59.95.

Lansky, the company that originated the angle-guide and clamp honing system, also offers other great sharpening products. Case in point is the Lansky Diamond Sharp Stick. The diamond-coated steel rod measures 9 inches overall and has a dual-molded ergonomic handle with a rubber gripping surface and sturdy plastic hand guard for safety.

A round sharpener such as this one makes quick

work of any blade shape and is especially adept at working on recurved blades since the rod follows the profiles perfectly. Only light pressure is needed for the sharpener to work effectively, as the grit is coarse for making quick work of larger blades. The rod is effective on many types of blades, from kitchen knives to large outdoor fixed blades as well as tactical knives. And when the job is done, the Diamond Sharp Stick can be hung on a hook thanks to a split ring that is threaded through a hole in the butt of the handle. With an MSRP of $33.99, the Lansky Diamond Sharp Stick is an affordable solution if you have multiple knives of fixed-blade and folding varieties.

I have used all these sharpeners to effectively hone super steels. Keep in mind that there are plenty more sharpeners on the market by these and other manufacturers that will do a great job at maintaining super steels. Select a sharpener based on your exact needs as well as budget, taking into consideration other features that make sharpeners easy to use.

Regardless of the sharpener selected and used for super steels, it is just a matter of altering your mindset when it comes to the frequency of blade maintenance. The more you maintain a blade, the better the original edge geometry is preserved. The longer you continue regular maintenance, the sharper the blade will be.

Plus, it will only take a couple minutes or so to maintain the edge as opposed to a long, drawn-out sharpening session that can eat up a good chunk of your time. Super steels are excellent for providing long-lasting edges, but there is a trade-off. They require more effort and time to sharpen when they become dull, so shift your mindset to edge maintenance rather than edge sharpening. That is the key to honing any super steel. □

FIN AND FEATHER KNIVES

The bird and trout test knives vary in both blade and handle styles, from left: Camillus Finscale Bird & Trout, White River Knife & Tool Small Game Knife and TOPS Knives Bird and Trout.

Pat Covert image

EDC FOLDERS

Four of the latest in EDC knives, from top to bottom: V Nives Killabite, Smith's Edgework-Site Wharncliffe Knife, Medford Knife & Tool Gentleman Jack and Pro-Tech Knives Malibu Wharncliffe.
ML Ayres image

A quartet of plucky linerlocks, from left: Puma SGB Mach 1, CRKT CEO Bamboo, Citadel Kampot and Steel Will Knives Nutcracker. *Marty Stanfield image*

KNIVES TO THE RESCUE

Three of the latest rescue knives, from left with manufacturer's suggested retail prices in parentheses: Hogue Knives First Response Trauma Tool Model 34760 ($180), Spyderco Assist Salt FRN Yellow ($170) and Utica Honor Rescue Blade ($29.50).

Abe Elias image

STICK YOUR NECK KNIVES OUT

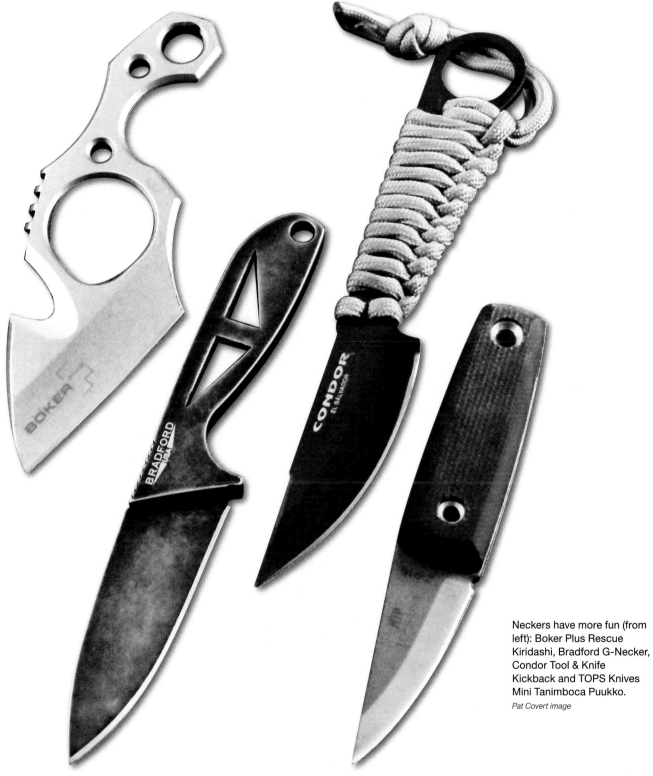

Neckers have more fun (from left): Boker Plus Rescue Kiridashi, Bradford G-Necker, Condor Tool & Knife Kickback and TOPS Knives Mini Tanimboca Puukko.

Pat Covert image

BUSHCRAFT IN THE U.S.A.

Four of today's top American-made bushcraft knives, from left: White River Knife & Tool Firecraft FC 3.5 Pro, TOPS Knives D Fly 4.5, Gerber Terracraft, and Camillus Bushcrafter.

Marty Stanfield image

COLOR THEM SHARP

A lot of color to be had in the cutlery world includes, from left: Steel Will Scylla Blue, Bear & Son 5-inch Pink Butterfly, Puma SGB Orange Featherweight Hunter and SOG-TAC CA Auto.

Pat Covert image

SINGULAR SPIKE TOMAHAWKS

Hot spike tomahawks, from right: Browning Shock 'N Awe, Cold Steel War Hawk, RMJ Tactical Knight Hawk and SOG Survival Hawk.

Marty Stanfield image

TACTICAL FIXED BLADES

According to V Nives owner and founder Mike Vellekamp, the main idea for the Frontier Survivor is as a "utilitarian-combat-survival crossover." "The three inches of stout, flat-ground bevel geometry toward the tip give it strength and toughness when piercing, thrusting and batoning, while the two inches of hollow-ground bevel toward the plunge make it great for fine cutting and whittling chores," he observed.

Metallurgist Jim Ankerson was looking to create a fixed blade that was a lightweight and sweetly balanced modification of the American bowie, a preferred style from his military days—and his collaborative design with Darrin Sanders, the Spyderco Province, was the result.

The Wayward Camper is the latest in the APOC line, delivering high performance with an overall length of 12.625 inches, blade length of 6.625 inches, weight of 14.5 ounces and MSRP of $89.

The KA-BAR Pocket Strike and its 3.1875-inch AUS 8A stainless steel hollow-ground blade, nylon fiberglass handle, and hard plastic sheath were constructed for the outdoors. MSRP: $67.21.

KNIFEMAKERS INDEX

BLADE SHOW

HELD ANNUALLY IN JUNE

FOR DETAILS VISIT

BLADESHOW.COM

CONNECT WITH US AT #BLADESHOW

HALFBREED
BLADES

AN EDGE ABOVE THE REST.

DELUXE SHARPENING SYSTEM

D-SHARP SHARPENER

Sharp knives at home or on the go. The Lansky Controlled-Angle System ensures that your knife edge is sharpened to the exact bevel you specify. Maintain your edge on the go with the all-new D-Sharp, featuring the same four angles as the Controlled-Angle System, for the perfect portable Sharpening accessory.

LEARN MORE AT LANSKY.COM

LANSKY®

▲ SHARPENERS

Sharpen your skills | Find us on 𝐟

BETTER KNIFE
BETTER LIFE

FRONT FLIPPER

GANNET QS137-C

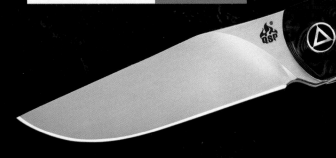

HAMSTER QS138-A

HAWK QS131-N

NO BATTLE RATTLE

SOLID LOCK-UP, NO BLADE RATTLE OPEN AND CLOSED

AUTO OTF
Large slide button for dependable automatic opening and closing.

DYNAMIC LOCKING SYSTEM
Provides secure blade lock-up and consistent and rapid opening.

CRYOGENICALLY HARDENED STEEL
CRYO S35VN
CRYO S35VN steel has superior edge retention and durability.

AMBIDEXTROUS DESIGN
Lightweight aluminum handle. Rugged and comfortable to hold and grip.

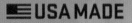 **USA MADE**

PENTAGON OTF

The first out-the-front knife in SOG's 35 years of existence is everything a demanding professional requires. The blade locks up quickly and securely. It doesn't loosen. It doesn't rattle. It doesn't need to be sent back to the factory for recalibration.

American-made, Pentagon OTF has a double-edged CYRO S35VN steel blade and incorporates a large, easy-to-engage, ambidextrous push-button opening mechanism as part of SOG's patented Dynamic Locking System.

It delivers confidence. Always.

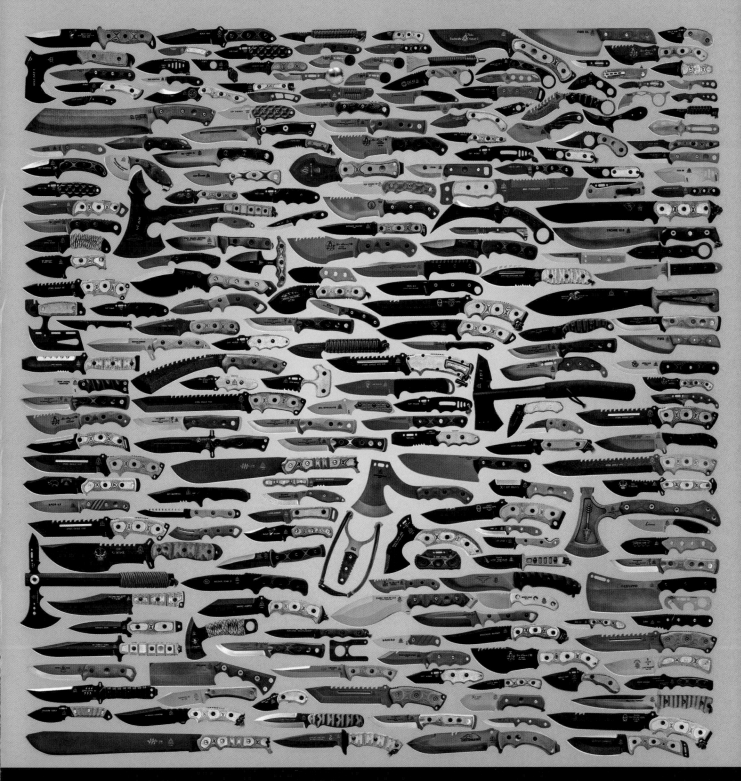

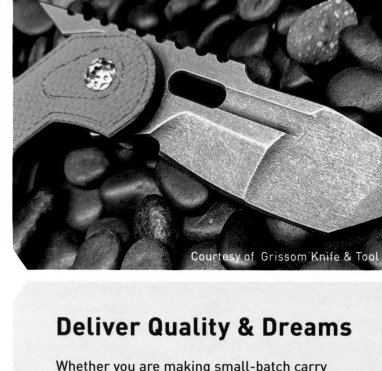

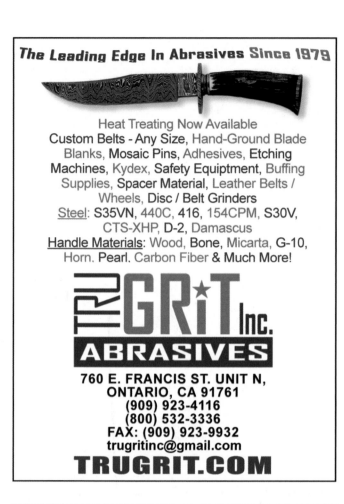

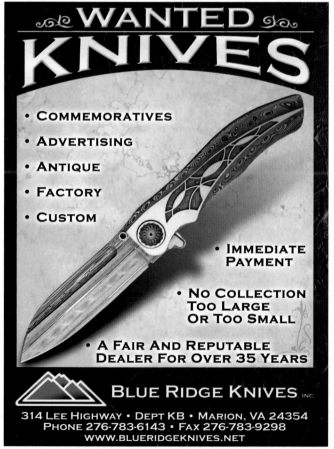

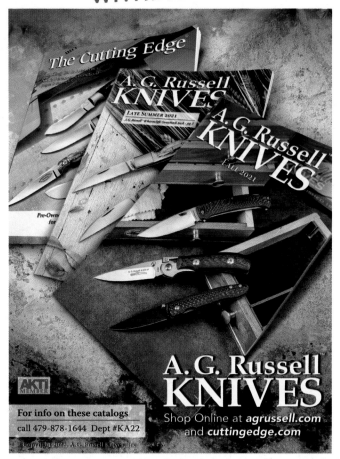
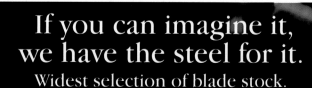
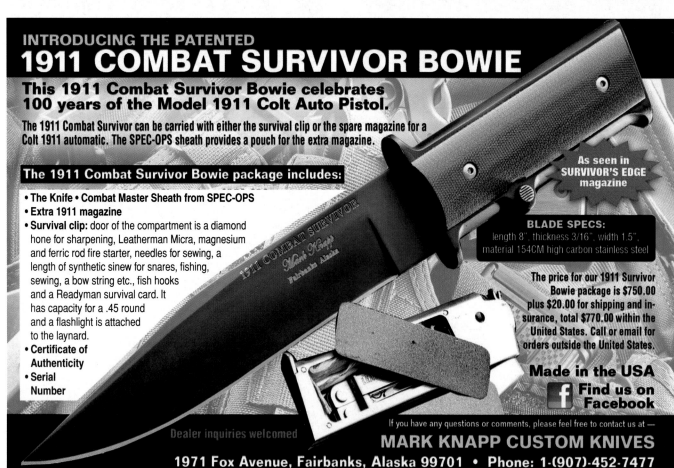